GREENISLAND PRESS

Also by Danny Morrison

NOVELS

West Belfast
On the Back of the Swallow
The Wrong Man
Rudi

NON-FICTION

Then The Walls Came Down
All The Dead Voices
Rebel Columns
Hunger Strike - Reflections (Ed.)
Life, I Do Not Understand You (book of
quotes & illustrations, Ed.)
The Comrades (Ed.)
*A Shared Struggle - Stories of Palestinian and
Irish Hunger Strikers* (Joint Ed.)

Free Statism
— & —
The Good Old IRA

Danny Morrison

GREENISLAND PRESS

This edition 2022
by
Greenisland Press
(Second revised and enlarged edition, November 2022)
e-mail: info@greenislandpress.ie
An imprint of Elsinor Verlag (Elsinor Press), Coesfeld, Germany
e-mail: info@elsinor.de
website: www.elsinor.de

Author contact – danny@dannymorrison.com
www.dannymorrison.com

Cover design by Seán Mistéil
Printed in Germany

ISBN 978-3-949573-00-2

In memory of Mick Timothy
(1948-1985)

Contents

Introduction

In August 1984, the late Mick Timothy, editor of *An Phoblacht/Republican News*, wrote one of his most incisive editorials, *Béal na mBláther*. It was in response to an oration given by Fine Gael Minister for Justice Michael Noonan speaking at Béal na mBláth, County Cork, where Michael Collins met his death early in the Civil War. Mick quite literally took Noonan at his word when he encouraged people to follow the example of Collins, 'the man who fought the Black and Tan terror until England was forced to offer terms'.

The power of that editorial resonates even to this day.[1]

---

[1] See Appendix 1, page 264

In 1985, I was the Director of Publicity for Sinn Féin. Brian McDonald, under the pen name Jack Madden, had earlier written a series of features attacking historical revisionism. He came to me at my Dublin office with an idea about a pamphlet. He and several others had been researching the guerrilla tactics of the Irish Republican Army against British Crown forces and their agents from 1919 to 1921 and were looking at the most common types of attacks: close-quarter killings of Royal Irish Constabulary policemen, whether on- or off-duty; the execution of informers; the assassinations of civil servants and magistrates; or operations that were bungled.[2]

These IRA activities made up a large proportion of attacks in what is referred to as the War of Independence or, colloquially, the Tan War. That war has been defended and commemorated—with different degrees of enthusiasm, opportunism, expediency, apathy or awkwardness—by Fianna Fáil and Fine Gael as the legitimate, justifiable deeds of a nation fighting to end British rule in Ireland.

Except, of course, the fighting didn't end British rule in Ireland.

Britain imposed partition as a *fait accompli* and created two states. Irish people whose hopes for Home Rule were

---

[2] See Appendices, Appendix 2, page 270

thwarted by Ulster Unionist threats of civil war, aided by British Army officers (*à la* Major General Henry Wilson and the 'Curragh Mutiny'), were transformed from being part of an oppressed majority into an oppressed minority in their own country.

The beneficiaries of partition were those who rose to power in the 'Southern area' (the expression used at the time even though it included Donegal, and was thereafter abbreviated to 'the South') and the Ulster Unionists in six of Ulster's nine counties. The oppressive conditions for nationalists in the North post-partition (socially, economically, politically and, moreover, existentially) were far worse and worse for far longer than the conditions generally prevailing in Ireland in the years immediately before Easter 1916. The Dublin slums had their comparative modern equivalents—27,000 occupied houses in Belfast unfit for human habitation in the 1960s. Rural poverty, working-class poverty and long-term unemployment (in some places up to fifty percent) were a feature of life for mainly nationalist people in places like Derry's Bogside and in Belfast's Ballymurphy. Some unionists experienced poverty and unemployment but on a lesser scale, sometimes on a marginally lesser scale in working-class areas like the Shankill and Sandy Row.

However low on the economic ladder, nationalists were always lower. The state of 'Northern Ireland' was and is a territory in which sectarianism is inbred.

Understandably, apologists for and advocates of any freedom struggle prefer to emphasise a narrative of the heroic—David versus Goliath; derring-do; the sacrifices; martyrdom; stories of Flying Columns and large-scale engagements; hunger strikes; ingenious escapes—and not the detail of the characteristically unseemly, quotidian side of small wars universally which are largely repugnant, even to the protagonists (which many memoirs often confessionally reflect).

In comparison to a hugely-experienced, modern-equipped British Army, the cutting edge of the British Empire, the Irish Republican Army of 1919 was poorly armed and lacked formal military training. Circumstances dictated that it fight an asymmetrical war, with whatever tactics it could, against superior numbers of professional, battle-hardened soldiers.

Throughout history during wartime, acts of heroism are accompanied also by cowardice and cruelty. Another universal fact is that civilians, by and large, bear the brunt of suffering. In conflicts, good people kill other good people for reasons of circumstance or because they are ordered to do so.

'In the end,' as the Vietnamese poet, Nguyen Duy, put it, 'in every war, whoever won, the people always lost.'

The German writer Thomas Mann wrote: 'It is nevertheless true that every war, even a war for humanity, does a good deal to soil, demoralize, brutalize, and stultify people.'

Timothy O'Grady (who co-authored *Curious Journey*, an oral history of interviews with IRA veterans of the Tan War) wrote in 2021:

'The war in Ireland like all wars had its examples of heroism, uncanny endurance, accidents and barbarisms. Most who participated in it thought they were doing what they had to do. The society does not in all cases find itself able to leap free from these events. The past keeps calling for a reckoning. This is obviously understandable, particularly for those who have not received answers, apologies or requests for forgiveness regarding their dead. But neurologists have demonstrated that you cannot remember unless you can also forget. It is equally true that total forgetfulness is itself a disease. It has further been demonstrated that acceptance and forgiveness are not only saintly, but also liberating. All of these qualities combine in an individual as a process rather than as something static, and perhaps also in societies. Some loyalists and some republicans sense the ameliorative effects of this. They would appear to be open to a more effective truth and reconciliation forum that was established in South Africa at the end of apartheid. This is less true of the British Government.'

As part of Féile an Phobail's 2021 August festival, I interviewed Susan McKay about her second book on unionism in the North, *Northern Protestants: On Shifting Ground*, which also challenges Irish republicans.

She said: 'There are villages in Fermanagh which have a high concentration of ex-security force people who moved back from the border. Republicanism would probably say, Well, the UDR was aligned in some cases with loyalist paramilitaries, was an anti-Catholic force, and so on. But there are people who were in the UDR who don't identify with that version of the UDR, who were driven out of their homes. People had to leave farms and things behind them. Their feeling of being exiled is real. They have as much right to their feelings about that as anyone else...

'The relatives of the victims of the Enniskillen bomb, their lives have been ruined by that. They are angry and bitter about the fact that they feel they never got justice any more than a lot of Catholic people got justice. I think that republicanism has to acknowledge, in a way it never has, that there was a strong strand of sectarianism in the republican campaign and it hasn't been admitted and it needs to be, and we have to go a lot deeper with legacy and reconciliation than we have done to date.'

In my reply I said: 'The big fear is that Truth and Reconciliation would consist of republicans telling all that they did and that then being pocketed. There would be no response from the other side. The UUP has never apologised and admitted to fifty years of rampant sectarian discrimination,' which along with violent state repression I hold as being the immediate trigger of the conflict.

It is deeply regrettable that warfare, above the influence of culture, fundamentally shapes the history of humanity and continues to define the world.

It is also deeply regrettable—but true—that if the issues which initially gave rise to conflict are unresolved in a settlement or compromise, inevitably a later generation, having endured the same or new injustices and frustrations, will become embroiled again in conflict, with all the tragedy and repetitions that involves.

In November 1972 the Taoiseach Jack Lynch said that Fianna Fáil was 'the direct descendant of the old IRA, the true IRA, which would have nothing to do with those who now claim to be the IRA.'

In publishing a selection of IRA operations from the Tan War period I knew that I risked unsettling romantic assumptions about the 'Good Old IRA' which Fianna Fáil and Fine Gael self-servingly perpetuate and rely upon to demonise the IRA of contemporary mainstream republicanism.

But I deemed it a worthwhile exercise.

To recognise similarities between the War of Independence period and the post-1968 'Troubles' era does not infer support for the modern IRA. What it does is facilitate an understanding of the *raison d'être* of the IRA from the early 1970s, how and why it flourished, endured, and came to be recognised as integral to any peace process.

Acknowledgement that the British war against the IRA had failed, and that there was a military stalemate, was important in seeding the peace process. In 1988, Sir James M. Glover, former General Officer Commanding the British Army in the North, said: 'In no way, can or will the Provisional Irish Republican Army ever be defeated militarily.' In 1992, a senior British Army officer in *The*

Times went further: 'the IRA is … better equipped, better resourced, better led, bolder and more secure against our penetration than at any time before. They are an absolutely formidable enemy. The essential attributes of their leaders are better than ever before. Some of their operations are brilliant…'

In later years, there were other admissions.

In 2004 the Scottish *Sunday Herald* published a briefing given by an MI5 officer, a former Royal Navy commander, at a maritime security conference on Orkney. The MI5 officer said the IRA had been 'the biggest threat to British national security' and 'in our opinion they have fought a just cause.' He said the conclusion of MI5 was 'based on the fact there had been legitimate grievances among, and discrimination against, the nationalist community and this had sustained the IRA through the length of the campaign… "Has it been a successful campaign?" The answer is yes.'

In July 2007, the BBC published an internal British Army document in which one military expert said that it had failed to defeat the IRA. It described the IRA as 'a professional, dedicated, highly skilled and resilient force'.

In May 2021, on the fortieth anniversary of the hunger strike, the BBC broadcast an interview with James Prior, former Secretary of State to the North, which was recorded two years before his death in 2014. The interviewer, veteran journalist Peter Taylor, asked Prior to reflect on the conflict and Prior replied:

'When one looks back in history, particularly our colonial history, one sees so many cases of where people who have fought us tooth and nail in every way that they could, eventually become rulers of those countries, and we accept them and talk to them, and get on with them...

'I didn't think there would ever be a time when the IRA was completely beaten and that therefore there would have to be some compromises made and that would lead on to Sinn Féin having power.'

Asked: 'Didn't the IRA strategy of the armalite and ballot box actually work?' he replied: 'I expect with the benefit of hindsight one has to say, it did - however unpleasant that sounds. I'm afraid it did win.'

The Good Old IRA, which has been out of print since the early 1990s, was principally aimed at Fianna Fáil and Fine Gael's contention that no comparisons were to be made between one struggle and another that had the same objectives, and which were separated merely by time. Their posture involves hypocrisy, inconsistency, double standards and an air of exceptionalism—our grandparents had the right to take up arms but you republicans in the North had no right to do so.

Put crudely: 'Our violence was good, yours bad.'

And: 'We can commemorate, you can't.'

Their demonisation of Sinn Féin has been relentless—if not ultimately pointless.

In 1984 Garret Fitzgerald established the New Ireland Forum to help the SDLP and prevent its support being eroded by Sinn Féin. Sinn Féin was excluded on the grounds that it 'supported violence'. Former SDLP member, the historian Dr Brian Feeney, described it thus: 'It sent the unequivocal message that the SDLP was the respectable northern party and Sinn Féin the pariah.' Similarly, Fitzgerald viewed the 1985 Anglo-Irish Agreement as a means of bolstering the SDLP and displaying the efficacy of constitutional politics.[3]

Unionists, on the other hand, who *also* supported violence, were invited to the Forum—though they refused to participate. Unionist politicians have never resiled from their position as cheerleaders for state violence and repression, curfews, internment, shoot-to-kill operations, the use of lethal plastic bullets; as defenders of RUC ill-

---

[3] *Sinn Féin—A Hundred Turbulent Years* by Brian Feeney, O'Brien.

treatment of suspects in interrogation centres; and supporters of harsh measures in the prisons. They flirted with loyalist paramilitaries, especially when they needed to mobilise street protests. Though unionist parties condemned loyalist violence it was often formulaic and with qualifications, including rationalising the loyalist sectarian assassination campaign.[4]

As Sinn Féin electorally overtook the SDLP in 2001, the invective from Fianna Fáil and Fine Gael became even more strident. With the rise of Sinn Féin in the Republic of

---

[4] Former Ulster Unionist Stormont Minister, John Taylor (now Lord Kilclooney) said in 1972: 'There is far too much talk about the handing in of guns… The time has come when the loyalists of Ulster must not give in to the campaign by Harold Wilson and the SDLP to disarm the law-abiding citizens of this province.' The same month he said: 'We should make it clear that force means death and fighting, and whoever gets in our way, whether republicans or those sent by the British Government, there would be killings.' In 1974 he said he would support the arming of loyalist paramilitaries 'with or without London government legislation.' About the GAA he said: 'I can understand why loyalist paramilitaries would attack the GAA as it is perceived as a political and divisive force.'
Unionist politicians, including Lord (Reg) Empey and Baron (David) Trimble sat on the Ulster Workers' Council (UWC) in 1974 allied to the UDA/UFF and the UVF (which, along with British agents, bombed Dublin and Monaghan, killing thirty three civilians and injuring three hundred others). In 1977 the DUP jointly organised a second UWC strike with the UDA whose members employed widespread violence. The DUP, of course, also formed Ulster Resistance whose members were involved in gun-running, many of their guns being used to kill hundreds of nationalists.

Ireland it has become hysterical. A battalion of historians, armchair historians, commentators, journalists and journalists-turned-advisors, in their vituperation have revealed themselves to be essentially defenders and proponents of partition. They are modern 'Free Staters'.

Some journalists repeatedly insult young voters with their paternalism. Telling them they are wrong about Sinn Féin, they can't understand the past because they are too immature—in their twenties, thirties or even their forties!

They accuse them of being naïve, that they have 'no memory of the murder and mayhem of the more recent Troubles' (Stephen Collins), have no idea of what the IRA did during the conflict—despite the media constantly reminding them. Arguably, there hasn't been another conflict anywhere in the world where the actions of the insurgents were more morally analysed for the human cost in suffering they inflicted than ours. These commentators, on the one hand, accuse republicans of playing down the bloodshed of the past, then, on the other, complain that Sinn Féin is glorifying the IRA and its past by revering the late Bobby Storey, or when someone shouts 'Up the Ra', or republicans commemorate dead IRA Volunteers.

If anyone plays down the bloodshed of the past it is those who glorify 'the good old IRA' by giving self-serving, revisionist orations at Béal na mBláth, where Collins was killed. Or Mícheál Martin speaking at a Liam Lynch commemoration, praising Lynch for putting 'pressure on the national leadership to allow volunteers to begin regular attacks on British forces... There are those who have tried to present Liam Lynch and those who stood with him as military fanatics marginal to the national victories of the time. This is a disgrace and complete misrepresentation of history.'

No mention in that speech of civilians killed in crossfire, or the shooting of fellow Irishmen in the RIC, or the disappearances and secret burial of informers, 'no memory of the murder and mayhem'.

Much has happened since this was first published in pamphlet form in 1985.

THE
GOOD
OLD
IRA

Tan War Operations

We have had a peace process, the ending of the IRA
military campaign in July 2005, decommissioning of
weapons, and huge political developments and shifts in
public opinion. But you would not know that if your world
was solely informed by Fianna Fáil and Fine Gael. In a way,
this publication is an updated riposte to their continuing
hypocrisy and double standards. And of how the more that
reunification becomes realisable, the more obstacles they
place in its way to maintain intact the Republic of Ireland—
which has its roots in the original Free State.

Fianna Fáil and Fine Gael could easily give speaking
rights in the Dáil to MPs from the North on issues which
affect their constituents. They refuse to properly plan for
constitutional change and establish a Citizen's Assembly, or
even a standing Oireachtas Committee on reunification.
Even when it comes to simple gestures they are completely
derelict. Given the opportunity to support the nomination
of northern unionist Ian Marshall to the Senate Fine Gael
put forward a party loyalist who was supported by Micheál
Martin and the Greens.

They have refused to open a dedicated Irish Passport
Office and citizen's advice facility in the North, despite the
unprecedented volume of applications. When will they
name a date for a referendum extending presidential voting

rights for citizens outside the Republic of Ireland? Or encourage sporting bodies in the South to ensure broadcasting rights to their games are negotiated on an all-Ireland basis to avoid the frustrating 'geo-block' on often important fixtures? When will they encourage even a very simple thing like broadcasters in the South (particularly the public broadcaster RTÉ) to lift the ban on audiences from the North entering competitions?

They lack any imagination and show no desire to move out of the *Free State* mindset.

In 2020 the Minister for Justice Charlie Flanagan's plan to commemorate those who tried to suppress the independence struggle was cancelled after a public outcry.

Modern Free Statism

Promotion of the idea that Ireland consists of twenty-six counties and that the nation stops at the Border

Fianna Fáil and Fine Gael politicians tell republicans that the terms 'Free State' and 'Free Stater' are pejorative and offensive, and that their usage is objectionable. I tend to agree and I can appreciate how it feels to have a term foisted on you which insults and does not reflect your identity. However, these are the very same people who have in recent years appropriated and consciously accentuated usage of the term 'Ireland' when they mean and can easily say the Republic of Ireland or the Republic.

They have no difficulty in deliberately offending and excluding the entire nationalist community of the North — Sinn Féin and SDLP supporters alike—from this definition of Ireland.

The original usage of the term *Ireland* was to *include* the Six Counties. Now it is used to *exclude* them.

The British-named *Free State* (*Saorstat Eireann*, consisting of twenty-six counties) was changed constitutionally by Fianna Fáil Taoiseach Éamon de Valera to *Eire* under the Constitution of Ireland Act, 1937.

Article 4 in the 1937 Constitution *does* say, 'The name of the State is Éire, or, in the English language, Ireland.' But that should be seen in the spirit of the Constitution's original (anti-partitionist) *all-Ireland* territorial claim in Article 2, in which the 'the national territory consists of the whole island of Ireland, its islands and the territorial seas'. Article 3 emphasised that the Constitution gave Saorstát Éireann the right to exercise jurisdiction over the whole of that territory.

When introducing legislation in December 1948 to change the name Éire to the Republic of Ireland (taking legal effect from Easter Monday 1949) An Taoiseach John A Costello replying to a question said, 'If the Senator will look at Article 4 of the Constitution she will find that the name of the State is *Éire*. Section 2 of this Bill declares that "this State shall be described as the Republic of Ireland." Its name in Irish is *Éire* and in the English language, Ireland. Its description in the English language is "the Republic of Ireland."'

In the text of the agreed communiqué at Sunningdale in 1973, the Republic is never referred to as 'Ireland'. In the Downing Street Declaration of 1993, Ireland is referred to as the whole 'island of Ireland' or 'people of Ireland, North and South'. The Good Friday Agreement does contain one reference to the 'Constitution of Ireland' and to Dublin representatives signing 'For the Government of Ireland'. There are also multiple mentions throughout of 'North/South' and to the 'island of Ireland'.

The term 'Ireland' (when referring to the Twenty-Six Counties) was never as habitually invoked as it has been since the signing of the Belfast (Good Friday) Agreement. The amendment of the territorial claim over the North as formerly expressed in Articles 2 and 3 does not justify the partitionist language of Dublin Government ministers. Article 2 now states: 'It is the entitlement and birthright of every person born in the island of Ireland, which includes its islands and seas, to be part of the Irish nation'. Article 3 includes, 'It is the firm will of the Irish nation, in harmony and friendship, to unite all the people who share the territory of the island of Ireland, in all the diversity of their identities and traditions…'

That this offensive nomenclature is clearly a deliberate choice by politicians is easily demonstrated. If they are to be consistent, relying on legalese to defend their usage of Ireland for the twenty-six county Republic of Ireland, then they should, but never do, refer to Londonderry which is the legal name for the city. A British High Court ruled in 2007 that the name could only be changed to Derry by Royal prerogative.

That such terminology is contentious was obvious from a very public airing which took place over a proposal to 'mark partition' in 2021. Michael D. Higgins had been invited to attend a church service in Armagh on 21 October. It was to be held in in St Patrick's (Church of Ireland) Cathedral. He declined to do so. Initially, the controversy was perceived to be over whether he had been properly addressed as the 'President of Ireland' rather than the 'President of the Republic' (the DUP's description) which he said he objected to as he was the President of *Ireland*—meaning not just the Twenty-Six Counties. However, after clarification that he had been properly addressed in the invitation he elaborated and said his objection was that the original invitation to a religious service had devolved into a political statement and thus it would be 'inappropriate' for him to attend.

The Armagh service had been organised to 'mark the centenaries of the partition of Ireland and the formation of Northern Ireland.' He said that in March he notified the organisers about his concerns that 'if this event is titled as it is, and structured as it is, it would present difficulties.'

He felt his concerns had not been taken on board. He did not attend.

Three years after the Belfast Agreement, Sinn Féin became the main voice of nationalists in the North. The impetus towards a Border referendum has been boosted by the repercussions of Brexit. Instead of recognising this, Southern politicians act to widen the partitionist gulf. They balk at the challenges of a reunification which may upset the status quo. It takes them out of a partitionist comfort zone.

In the years before the IRA ended its armed struggle, statements from various political parties and church leaders emphasised how republicans would be free to pursue their aspirations and objectives, campaign and agitate for a united Ireland. Republicans never viewed the Good Friday Agreement as being the end of the story but as part of a process for reversing partition and ending British interference in Irish affairs. Unionists, quite understandably, oppose this impetus.

Micheál Martin, in 2020, as Taoiseach and leader of
Fianna Fáil, went so far as to describe a referendum on
unity—as provided by the Good Friday Agreement—as
'divisive' and 'partisan' and one that won't be carried out on
his watch.[5]

This dismayed many in Fianna Fáil's grassroots who aspire
to reunification. All major policy differences generate
division. That was the case with divorce, gay marriage and
abortion proposals which were settled through referenda.
Why should the debate about partition be different?
Proposing an all-Ireland health service, free at the point of
delivery, might be a partisan step too far for the Fianna Fáil
leaders, though I doubt if it would be north of Dundalk and
east of Letterkenny.

When it comes to Sinn Féin, Fianna Fáil and Fine Gael
have never ceased fire, have never entered into a
rapprochement. Where is the spirit of reconciliation that

---

[5] There was an interesting spat between Leo Varadkar and Micheál
Martin in December 2017 when Varadkar said, 'no Irish government
will ever again leave Northern nationalists and Northern Ireland
behind.' Martin found the remark 'offensive' and a slur on Fianna Fáil's
record. In 2021 at the Fine Gael ard fheis Varadkar, again perhaps
exposing Martin's half-heartedness, said he believes 'in the unification of
our island and I believe it can happen in my lifetime.' Of course, he also
felt the need to attack Sinn Féin, the main engine behind constitutional
change, for its 'crude vision' which he described as a 'a cold form of
republicanism, socialist, narrow nationalism, protectionist, anti-British,
euro-critical, ourselves alone, 50 per cent plus one and nobody else is
needed.'

republicans in the North were exhorted to show at difficult times in the peace process? Fianna Fáil and Fine Gael are arrogant, elitist, virtuous and precious. They demanded after the 2017 collapse of the Assembly at Stormont that Sinn Féin get back into an administration with the Democratic Unionist Party in the North whilst simultaneously declaring Sinn Féin an unfit coalition partner in the South. In 2020 after the general election if there was one major issue upon which Fianna Fáil and Fine Gael agreed it was to exclude Sinn Féin from government.

'Our violence was good, yours bad.'

Language in relation to describing the Irish state, the 'Northern Ireland' territory and the relationship between Britain and Ireland reflects a degree of ambiguity. There is one sovereign state in Ireland, confined to twenty-six counties, and two administrations based in Dublin and Belfast, one of which, in the North, is subordinate, under 'United Kingdom' sovereignty. Unlike the Scottish nation, which is part of Great Britain, the northern Irish territory, which is not part of Great Britain, does not and cannot exercise self-determination. That right is reserved for all the people of Ireland (or peoples, if you prefer) at a time when a majority in the Six Counties opt for it.

Unionists self-identifying as British, or insisting that 'Northern Ireland is as British as Finchley', complain that there is a nationalist cultural war on their 'Britishness' which is, in fact, merely the cut and thrust of politics and contested narratives. However, their 'Britishness' is contradicted day and daily by British Government policies (the latest being the Protocol and an EU border down the Irish Sea). The lack of affinity is also reflected in the British public's attitudes expressed in opinion polls, and ultimately their disinterest in the North.

In October 2019 the staunchly Tory newspaper the *Daily Telegraph* carried a feature which said: 'Northern Ireland is a burden on the rest of the UK. We can't let it get in the way of Brexit… Northern Ireland has long been a millstone round the neck of the rest of the UK and to fail to take back our independence because of it would be an historic tragedy.'

A host of other factors—historical, social, political, cultural—also differentiate unionists (and nationalists) of the North from the people of England and Scotland. No referendum in Finchley—not even one carried by a hundred percent—can take its residents out of the UK, whereas a simple majority in the North can.

Integration, accommodation and the emergence of a hybrid communal identity on this island would have been a consequence of the passage of time and of peaceful coexistence had the imposition of partition—which was never meant to be permanent—not prevented that.

Fianna Fáil and Fine Gael attempts to deliberately conflate the Republic of Ireland with Ireland is to create the perception that the Republic of Ireland *is* the nation and that the North is 'other'. If politicians in the South are truly opposed to partition, why engage in terminological partitioning and psychological conditioning? Why deliberately offend the very people who were historically sacrificed so that you could enjoy your freedom?

Commenting after securing his second term in office in 2018, President Michael D. Higgins, in part a response to the extremely divisive campaign of his opponent Peter Casey, said: 'Words matter. Words can hurt. Words can heal. Words can empower. Words can divide.'

'Othering' manifests itself in many, sometimes ugly, ways. Belfast-born President Mary McAleese was earlier pigeonholed as a republican supporter, notwithstanding her opposition to the IRA's armed struggle, when she worked in RTÉ. It was because she expressed views on the North from a lived nationalist experience. Her objective and accurate journalistic assessments—for example that Bobby Sands would win the Fermanagh & South Tyrone by-election in 1981—were contrary to the prevailing orthodoxy, for which she was shouted down and ridiculed. That orthodoxy was based on a ruthless censorship. McAleese observed: 'How many of these people, if you were to ask them: "How much time have you spent there [in the North]? Do you know what it was like to live there? Did you ever sit down and have a conversation with me for example about living there?" No, they did not. They hadn't a clue … I was always bemused by the cluelessness of people who talked as if they were experts and who got away with it.'

During McAleese's successful 1997 bid to be elected President of Ireland, as a Fianna Fáil candidate, she was subjected to gratuitously vitriolic comments from commentator Eoghan Harris, who had been an enthusiastic supporter of 'Section 31' state broadcasting censorship in RTÉ. He called McAleese a 'tribal time-bomb'. He later went on to become an advisor to Ulster Unionist Party leader David Trimble, before morphing into a post-1998, pro-unionist Fianna Fáil adviser and cheerleader. Harris's anti-Sinn Féin views are not unique. A rival candidate to McAleese said she wasn't a 'proper' person for the role.

MacEoin and McGuinness

When Fianna Fáil entered government in 1932, Éamon de Valera appointed Frank Aiken, from Camlough, South Armagh, as Defence Minister. Ten years earlier, on 17 June 1922, Aiken, as leader of the Fourth Northern Division, was associated with an IRA operation in the village of Altnaveigh, in which six Protestant loyalists, including a husband and wife, were killed in reprisal for a rape and the killing of nationalists by the B-Specials (Ulster Special Constabulary police reservists). It is not something on which Aiken reflected or commented upon in later life and it is not something his leader, Éamon de Valera, insisted he speak about. That is unlike demands made of Sinn Féin leaders today by current Fianna Fáil leader Micheál Martin.[6]

IRA actions throughout the Tan War led to civilian casualties. For instance, in an attack in 1921 on a train at Upton, eight civilians, including railwaymen, were shot dead, and three IRA Volunteers killed, after the IRA opened fire on British soldiers on the train.

---

[6] Patrick Casey, a Vice-Brigadier in the IRA, later said: 'I was surprised at the time that Frank Aiken had planned and authorised this.' Aiken never repudiated the attacks, which were generally perceived to be sectarian. Casey was also critical of Aitken for cancelling Armagh and South Down Brigades' participation in a rising in the Six Counties in the Spring of 1922, the withdrawal of the Brigades freeing up Crown Forces which facilitated the suppression of the areas that went ahead.

In targeted attacks on military personnel, women—either wives or girlfriends—accompanying soldiers or policemen were also accidentally killed.

In the Tan War the IRA killed almost five hundred policemen of the Royal Irish Constabulary. As leader of a much-feared IRA Flying Column in Longford in 1920, Seán MacEoin was engaged in daring and dangerous confrontations with British forces. Indeed, he was wounded, captured and sentenced to death. Among the many deaths he was responsible for were the killing of twenty-three-year-old Philip Kelleher from Cork who had been four months in the RIC; forty-five-year-old Constable Peter Cooney, a married man, shot in the back whilst returning from leave; and thirty-year-old RIC District Inspector Thomas McGrath, a single man from County Limerick, shot through the head when he knocked on the door of the house MacEoin was staying in.

At MacEoin's funeral in July 1973 Bishop—later Cardinal—Cahal Daly erased the death of Thomas McGrath and others and instead emphasised MacEoin's wartime chivalry in caring for enemy wounded before becoming committed to peace; praised him for being a good Catholic who prayed daily, and stated that he never besmirched the cause by cowardice or inhumanity.

'Wherever green is worn, indeed wherever men cherish freedom, or the oppressed struggle to be free, the name of General Sean MacEoin will be remembered in honour, with pride and with affection,' said Daly. 'He was among Ireland's bravest and noblest fighters for freedom. He is remembered for a courage that is rightly legendary.'

MacEoin and his comrades shot and bombed British soldiers and RIC policemen, civil servants, magistrates, agents and informers. They killed them wherever they could find them—on holiday, out for a stroll, on leave, in bed with their wives, at their dinner tables, having a drink at the bar, on patrol, or at their barracks. Fine Gael is proud of IRA men like MacEoin. After all, his and other IRA killings and the sacrifices of the patriot dead brought them to power.

In 1945, Fine Gael put forward Seán MacEoin for the Irish Presidency. Now, contrast Fine Gael and Fianna Fáil's attitude to Martin McGuinness, Deputy/Joint First Minister in the Northern Executive, when he ran for the Presidency of Ireland in 2011, *seventeen years* after the ceasefire and *six years* after the formal end of the IRA's campaign. Their attitude reinforced the barriers faced initially by Mary McAleese. Fine Gael declared, as with McAleese, that McGuinness was unfit to run for public office.

Martin McGuinness had stood in elections in the North, been elected an MP and Member of the Legislative Assembly, worked for the peace process (including bringing lessons that he learned in Ireland to Iraq, the Basque Country and Sri Lanka); and had worked for a ceasefire, IRA decommissioning and the devolution of justice and peace. He was Minister for Education and Deputy/Joint First Minister with the Democratic Unionist Party leaders Ian Paisley, Peter Robinson and Arlene Foster. He stood shoulder-to-shoulder with the Police Service of Northern Ireland after the killings of its officers, a stance for which his life was threatened. He represented the Northern Executive on trade missions to the USA and the European Union which attracted millions of pounds in investment.

Fine Gael ministers, including party leader and Taoiseach Enda Kenny, sat with Martin McGuinness on the North-South Ministerial Council for years without demur. No one in Fine Gael queried his worthiness—until, that is, he decided to stand for the Irish presidency. Good enough to govern with unionists, but not for the good people of the Republic.

'Our violence was good, yours bad.'

On social media, and even in an RTÉ election programme, Fine Gael supporters, no doubt fortified by their leadership's attacks on the late Deputy/Joint First

Minister, told McGuinness, 'Go back to your own country!'

Fine Gael's querying of McGuinness as an 'appropriate candidate' was, of course, mere expediency. When it suited Fine Gael the party went into government in 1948 with the 1930s Chief of Staff of the IRA, Seán MacBride, in order to oust Fianna Fáil. As part of the coalition government agreement with MacBride's Clann na Poblachta party, it also agreed to amnesty IRA prisoners. This included my Uncle Harry who had been sentenced to death for the killing of Detective Garda George Mordaunt in 1942.

Ironically, Fianna Fáil's vilification of Sinn Féin is not dissimilar to the Fine Gael precursor, Cumann na nGaedheal's scare tactics against Fianna Fáil as this front page advertisement (next page) on the day of the general election on 16 February 1932, shows.

Interestingly, the advertisement quotes Tipperary Fianna Fáil candidate Dan Breen, speaking in Borrisoleigh on 14 February, 1932. Breen does not balk at what 'the Good Old IRA' did during the Tan War:

'It is said we killed people. We did kill. Killing is a hard thing, and we make no apology for what we have done, and if circumstances arose we would kill again. It is said we took money from the banks. There were millions in the coffers of the Bank of Ireland, and who had a better right to it than the men who were fighting for their country.'

Irish republicanism in its quest to end the disastrous role of Britain in Irish affairs reminds Fine Gael and Fianna Fáil that they are products of different stages of resistance and freedom struggle defeated (in the case of the pro-Treaty Free Staters, 1922) or abandoned (by Fianna Fáil, 1926). Those parties justify their separate stances over the bloody Civil War but agree on the morality of the guerrilla war against Britain which preceded it.

In the Civil War, the Free State leadership was ruthless. The Public Safety Act of September 1922, a month after the death of General Michael Collins at Béal na mBláth, empowering military courts to carry out reprisal killings of republican prisoners, ensured that there could be no going back, no room for compromise among former comrades. The Free Staters executed fifty-three more prisoners than the British during the independence struggle. More than 11,000 republicans and their supporters were imprisoned, many brutalised whilst incarcerated. Seventy-seven republicans in total were executed and many others were summarily shot in extra-judicial killings, which also included tying prisoners to mined barricades and blowing them to pieces at Ballyseedy Cross, Countess Bridge and at Cahirciveen, County Kerry, in March 1923—a total of seventeen prisoners dying in such a manner.

In November 1922 Free State soldiers, using a British Army Crossley tender, trained their Lewis machine gun on an open air meeting of the Republican Prisoners Defence Committee on O'Connell Street, attended mostly by women. They opened fire and killed Lily Bennett and seriously wounded seven others, including newsboy Michael Leaden. 'His condition,' said the *Irish Times*, 'was very serious, and no hopes were entertained of his recovery.'

After Collins's death William Cosgrave became chairman of the Provisional Government. He said: 'I am not going to hesitate and if the country is to live and if we have to exterminate 10,000 republicans, the three millions of our people are bigger than the ten thousand.'

The 'exterminator' later led Fine Gael from 1934 until 1944.

Imagine if this energy and commitment had, at the time, been put into confronting Britain and British forces over partition instead of killing Irish men and women who remained loyal to the oath they had taken to uphold the Republic as declared in 1916?

Prior to the Civil War, in 1922, Michael Collins despaired of unionist refusal to end its pogroms and to reinstate thousands driven from their work in the shipyards and in other employments. Sensing no unionist intention to abandon sectarianism as a method of ruling the partitioned territory, Collins planned a unified offensive against the Six-County regime. Before and even after the start of the Civil War, arms and explosives were supplied to anti-Treaty republicans. Explosives destined for the campaign exploded after Free State troops set fire to the Four Courts, occupied by the IRA, in the opening act of the Civil War in June 1922.

Collins's attack on the Four Courts resulted from British outrage directed at anti-Treaty forces after republicans assassinated Field Marshal Sir Henry Wilson in London, probably on orders from Collins. Playing two ends against the middle ended disastrously for Collins. The attack on the North failed, not least due to an intensifying civil war in the Free State. With Collins's death at Béal na mBláth in August 1922, Free State and subsequent administrations ceased to provide material help to nationalists under sectarian attack, until the Arms Crisis debacle of 1970.[7]

---

[7] As a Major-General based in the Curragh Military Camp in 1914, Henry Wilson sided with the unionists, the UVF and Westminster Opposition leaders to weaken and depose the Liberal government over Home Rule. He and other officers threatened to resign rather than enforce the law in Ulster, thus strengthening the unionist cause. During the Tan War he favoured greater repression—and threatened to resign if Kevin Barry's death sentence was commuted—and was opposed to peace talks. He became MP for Down and was Sir James Craig's military advisor. Collins held him responsible for the anti-nationalist pogroms of 1921-1922.

Fianna Fáil, having split from Sinn Féin in 1926, gradually slotted into the twenty-six-county framework and comfortably adopted a Free State psyche—that the nation stopped at Dundalk, that the state had no responsibilities towards the North. Fianna Fáil has always been a partitionist party. Had it been serious about uniting the country it would have organised in the Six Counties and could have facilitated Northern representation in the South. (Éamon de Valera did stand on an abstentionist ticket and was elected in South Down for Fianna Fáil, but that was a token gesture.) Instead, it excoriates the party which the nationalist community has democratically chosen as its preferred representatives and refuses to engage on the pressing issue of the national question.

Fianna Fáil leader Micheál Martin is disingenuous when he calls on Sinn Féin's elected representatives to account for those involved in IRA actions during the most recent conflict—which ended over a quarter of a century ago. Was Fianna Fáil founder and leader Éamon de Valera accountable for the actions of Fianna Fáil member Timothy Coughlan, one of those responsible for the 1927 assassination of Kevin O'Higgins TD, Free State Minister for Home Affairs? Two years before his killing O'Higgins was being harangued by republicans at a public meeting in Sligo about the executions.

He answered, unapologetically, 'I stand by the seventy-seven executions – and 774 more if necessary.'

On Sunday, 10 July 1927, three anti-Treaty members of the IRA, including Fianna Fáil member Coughlan, fatally wounded O'Higgins as he made his way to mass. In fact, rather than distance the party from the assassin, Fianna Fáil named a cumann after him which was still active in the 1980s.

Martin's call in relation to the more recent conflict is in a context where no British Government will account for its murderous sectarian collusion with and direction of loyalist killers. (During his investigations, former London Metropolitan Police chief Lord Stevens and his team arrested 210 paramilitary suspects, of whom, he said, 207 were registered agents or informants for the British state.)

Martin will not even press the British to accede to repeated motions from the Dáil in support of a call for co-operation from Judge Barron investigating the mass killings of Irish citizens in the 1974 Dublin and Monaghan bombings. Bloody Sunday, a mass murder of civil rights marchers by the British Army's elite Parachute Regiment in broad daylight, resulted after fifty years and massive international pressure, and two expensive inquiries, in the charging of just one former low-ranking soldier. He is a token of Britain's contempt for due process, as it concerns its

Irish wars. That appears to be good enough for Micheál Martin, who imposes a different, more stringent, standard on Sinn Féin.

On the day that an inquest declared that the ten civilian victims of the 1971 Ballymurphy Massacre were completely innocent, British Prime Minister Boris Johnson signalled the introduction of an amnesty for military veterans, thus completely reneging on the pledges contained in the 2014 British/Irish Stormont House Agreement on legacy, which provided for human rights compliant investigations with full accountability for all sides. Thousands of republicans had already served lengthy periods of imprisonment but very few official agents of the state, all of whom were protected, had gone to jail. But the indefatigable campaigns by relatives and their lawyers had brought to a point the prosecutions and prospective successful convictions of British soldiers, intelligence officers and their agents who had been given carte blanche to murder.

In July 2021 the British Government announced plans to introduce legislation which would protect its soldiers and agents from further legal scrutiny and investigation by way of a general amnesty. The amnesty would end prosecutions for any conflict-related actions which occurred prior to the 1998 Belfast Agreement, would end inquests, Police

Ombudsman investigations, and end all civil litigation by families or victims of judicial injustice such as internees or those falsely convicted.

Justice and the truth are inextricably linked.

Given the cover-ups over decades, we know only some of what the British Government was involved in and responsible for.

In November 2005 in a feature in *Daily Ireland* I predicted that once the paper trail on the dirty war got close to Number 10 Downing Street the British Government would act. I said: 'Despite the many obstacles placed in their [families' and relatives'] way, the campaigns and some of the inquiries for the truth about state violence have revealed the black nature of Britain's dirty war and its collusion in the loyalist assassination campaign.

'The only ones who can implicate British ministers in the dirty war are those in the intelligence services who reported to them. Were they ever to face the prospects of prosecution they would be sure to threaten to bring down with them their political masters. It is then that the British Government will issue a comprehensive amnesty.

'Not out of a sense of justice. Not for peace, reconciliation or as part of conflict resolution.

'But to ensure that it has got away with murder.'

Culture and Media

The partitionist mentality of politicians in the Republic of Ireland can also be seen among those who consider themselves progressive. Their passion for human rights or national liberation is in direct proportion to the distance oppression is from home, the farther the revolutionary struggle is from Ireland. It can be seen among some historians, academics and journalists also. It seeps into all aspects of life, including cultural representation.

In his 'Introduction to *The Penguin Book of Irish Fiction*', the cultural revisionist Colm Tóibín singled out for special mention John Banville's 1973 novel *Birchwood*: 'the most radical text in Irish revisionism', he tells us. He extols it for making 'fun of rebellion and land wars and famine, Irish myths of origin which had been dear to the hearts of the founding fathers'. According to Tóibín, 'Ireland' needs to rid itself of the burden of history, ditch nationalism and embrace Europe. Of course, Tóibín's 'Ireland' is twenty-six of its thirty-two counties. A united Ireland is 'a matter of indifference to most people in the Republic', he proclaims, speaking for himself. Cracking a joke about the Famine, like one about the Holocaust, betrays, in an Irish context, the reactionary basis of revisionist understanding.

Tóibín accurately summed up the purpose of revisionist

historical research when he observed, in another essay, that it was 'precisely what our state needed once the North blew up … in order to isolate Northern Ireland from us and our [*sic*] history … [Roy] Foster and his fellow historians' work became useful, not for its purity, or its truth, but its politics'.

Tóibín's radical texter, Banville, criticised critics who apparently regard Foster with 'venom'. Foster, he wrote in the *London Review of Books* (July 2015), is 'one of the finest contemporary Irish historians'. His 'magisterial and subtle' *W. B. Yeats: A Life* provoked 'nationalist wrath', he said, for no reason, apart from 'the fact that Foster is a Protestant Irishman who lives and works in England'. These caricatures expose the vacuity of revisionist understanding, in this case while contemplating the life of a Protestant nationalist and sometime republican, W. B. Yeats.

The truth about revisionists, however, is that their purported objective stance is really partitionist and anti-republican, it has supplied no answers and does not challenge the injustices which are at the core of our conflict.

The men and women of 1916 and the Tan War period had, like all of us, feet of clay. But they were sincere revolutionaries, deserving of respect. It is disingenuous and ahistorical to lump them and their memory in with the reactionary politics that subsequently emerged. Literary and then political censorship, Magdalene Laundries, Mother & Baby Home scandals, abuse of children in institutional settings, illegal adoptions, bans on contraception, divorce and, later, abortion, which variously affected both parts of Ireland, all illustrate the 'carnival of reaction' James Connolly predicted that partition would produce.

A great deal of what emerged was a product of colonial administration during the nineteenth century, as Roman Catholicism was promoted to combat revolutionary republican ideas, and as Protestantism retreated from legal privilege across the island to enforced sectarian rule, based on numerical superiority, in the North.

From 1972 until the peace process, censorship prevented many unpalatable truths from being aired. Republicans and entire nationalist communities were demonised. For two decades RTÉ's Section 31's censorship, politically and deliberately distanced the state and the people from the northern nationalist community, a community sacrificed to partition so that Twenty-Six Counties could be free.

But censorship was only part of the atmosphere of repression in the South, particularly during the Fine Gael/Labour coalition government of 1973-1977. It announced a state of emergency and its ministers turned a blind eye to Gardaí abuses of detainees. There was a general increase in harassment of those who supported nationalists in the North, and harsher conditions for republican prisoners which triggered hunger strikes.

The 'systematic maltreatment' of detainees (Amnesty International report) resulted in miscarriages of justice in complicit, special non-jury courts, with innocent people convicted on the sole basis of false confessions beaten out of them by a group of detectives who became known as the 'heavy gang'. During one interrogation in Cahir Gardaí station a victim, Thomas Connors, tried to commit suicide by jumping through a window.

Reports of brutality were consistently rejected by the Garda Síochána and coalition government ministers. Such was the climate of fear that as the accounts became irrefutable questions were asked how this could have happened. Journalists stated that even doctors were reluctant to examine victims and become implicated and solicitors were loath to issue summons they were so afraid for their careers. Even victims—those released without being charged—were afraid to complain in case they suffered further intimidation and harassment. And how was that climate of fear created and sustained? In the same way that Section 31 was policed within RTÉ. By accusing anyone who complained as being republican sympathisers who were spreading republican propaganda. Those making allegations, said Fine Gael TD Gerard Lynch, 'came from one of two sources… those engaged in anti-State activities and their admirers from different walks of life.'[8]

Patrick Cooney, Minister for Justice, said that those 'who expressed concern' about Garda brutality 'were not as quick to condemn subversives.' He rejected calls that those detained should have medical attention because it implied they would need such attention.

Cooney was arrogance personified. He said: 'If those who made such calls were consistent they would also require access to hairdressers, dentists and opticians for people held in custody.'

When asked if he would ask the Garda Commissioner about the allegations of a 'heavy gang' Cooney said, 'there is no need to ask the Garda Commissioner about such allegations as that would imply that it was official policy to have such a squad in existence.'

In February 1976 Cooney was the minister responsible for ordering the plane carrying the body of hunger striker Frank Stagg to be directed to Shannon and away from Frank's waiting mother and siblings at Dublin Airport. He

---

[8] One of the best books on this period is *Round Up the Usual Suspects* by Gene Kerrigan and the late Derek Dunne, *Magill* 1984.

was also responsible for the burial of Frank's body in an unmarked grave which was subsequently sealed with four tonnes of concrete to prevent Frank's supporters from burying him in the Republican Plot in Ballina which were his dying wishes (and which was subsequently realised in 1977).

But Cooney was not without support in the mainstream media. This is how a disgusting and heartless editorial in the *Irish Times* justified the hijacking of Frank's remains: 'It may seem harsh to say it, but in this case neither the wishes of the family, nor of the dead man himself are paramount. What is being denied is not a decent and orderly burial, but the opportunity for men of clearly subversive intent to exploit to the last the death of the hunger-striker. The over-riding consideration is the government's duty to maintain security and to preserve its authority.'

That was exactly the same justification given by the British Government in 1920 when it diverted the remains of hunger striker Terence Mac Swiney from Dublin where plans had been made for a huge funeral procession from the capital to Cork city with towns and villages able to pay their respects.

The *Irish Times* also had no difficulty with publishing year after year distasteful columns by Kevin Myers in which republicans were demonised. In one such appalling column he described dead IRA Volunteers as 'the progeny of a sow's litter.'

State censorship has been applied to all aspects of the life of republicans. Workers at Gateaux Bakery in Dublin in 1990 elected Larry O'Toole (a member of Sinn Féin), to be their spokesperson during a strike. After an RTÉ interview with O'Toole, Joe Mulholland, head of news, stepped in and banned him, citing Section 31 of the Broadcasting Act, telling O'Toole that RTÉ will not interview any person from Sinn Féin on any topic under any circumstances. They had already taken off the air, in mid-conversation, the late Paddy Wright, a Sinn Féin Councillor, who was participating in a programme about gardening. O'Toole, at great expense, took his case to the High Court which found in July 1992 that Mulholland's directive was an illegal extension of censorship. Instead of welcoming this increase in editorial freedom RTÉ appealed the ruling to the Supreme Court, and lost the appeal. O'Toole accused RTÉ of having 'taken up the cudgels on behalf of the government.'

Of course, the same censorship was never enacted against spokespersons for the Workers Party which maintained an armed wing after its so-called ceasefire and many of whose members were also in influential positions in RTÉ.[9]

Vestigial Stalinists of that party are still occasionally seen and heard though it is difficult to keep up with the innumerable parties they have moved in and out of. Leading revisionist guru Eoghan Harris was disgraced and stripped of his column in the *Sunday Independent* in May 2021 when it was revealed that he was behind bogus Twitter accounts (including one in which he called himself Barbara J. Pym) which targeted, demonised and harangued Sinn Féin members and harassed journalists, particularly women, whom he thought weren't tough enough on republicans or obsequious to unionists and sympathetic to their dilemmas.

The portrayal of the republican struggle as atavistic, reactionary and the product of an inexplicable nationalism which spawned mindless violence was constant. The revisionists became so arrogant and unrestrained that they felt in 2001 they could attack the re-interment of Kevin Barry and nine other IRA Volunteers in Glasnevin Cemetery, men who had been court-martialled and executed by British forces in 1920–1921.

---

[9] Writing in the *Irish Times* on 23 April, 2021, the former leader of the Workers Party Proinsias De Rossa described the aspiration for unity as 'nineteenth-century intellectual baggage' and continued: 'It is a common part of our public discourse in the Republic of Ireland to say one agrees with, wants, or supports the idea of a "united Ireland". But why? Why is this necessary?'

'Why could they not be exhumed and reburied in private?' plaintively asked *The Sunday Times*. The funerals, wrote Fintan O'Toole in *The Irish Times*, will offer 'a great boost to those who want us to feel that the only difference between a terrorist and a patriot is the passage of time'.

'Like the Americans of today,' wrote Paddy Murray in the *Sunday Tribune*, equating 'the murderous deeds' of the Volunteers of the War of Independence with the jihadist suicide bombers who flew into the World Trade Centre, 'they [the British] demanded retribution. Kevin Barry and nine others provided that retribution with their deaths.'

Kevin Myers, also in *The Irish Times*, complained that the event was all about reaffirming 'a single narrative of suffering and sacrifice'.

Such commentators want nationalist Ireland to feel guilty about its past, without begging the same moral question of Britain and unionists about their disastrous roles. The funerals, they said, 'are sending a dangerous signal to impressionable young people' and 'will be widely and dangerously misunderstood'. What they actually believe but are reluctant to say aloud is that 'the people are stupid; we must save them from themselves'.

Labour Party leader Ruairi Quinn said that the funerals were a cynical exploitation by Fianna Fáil, aimed at stealing Sinn Féin's clothes and minimising its rival's electoral advances. After all, Fianna Fáil had ample opportunity to exhume the bodies during its many lengthy periods of government, especially in 1966 during the golden jubilee of the 1916 Rising. It chose to leave them lying in prison yards. At any stage, even during the recent conflict, it could have released the remains to the next-of-kin but chose not to. Whatever about the timing of the reburials, for most people, including Fianna Fáil supporters, the funerals represented a recognition of patriots who sacrificed their lives in the struggle for independence. It was the right thing to do, however late.

What many of the opponents of the funerals resented was the fact that the event tapped into a buoyant public mood that they had strived to repress over a number of decades. It demonstrated their failure.

It is the parallels they really fear. What is the difference between Kevin Barry executed by the British in 1920 and Kevin Barry O'Donnell executed by the British in 1992? The sectarian conditions under which the British ruled all of Ireland were intensified and recodified in the North after 1920. Kevin

Barry O'Donnell fought under those less favourable conditions and also paid for his sacrifice with his life.[10]

Scalpel 31 of the Broadcasting Act. 2017 RTÉ map of 'Ireland' disappears 1.8m people and creates a new coastline for surfers and trawlers in Cavan and Monaghan.

The Centenary

In 2016, the Department of Arts, Heritage and the Gaeltacht's first foray into commemorating the Easter Rising as part of the Decade of Centenaries was quite telling. The Irish Government department produced a video which did not include any mention of the Rising or of the executed

---

[10] Kevin Barry O'Donnell (aged 21) was killed with three IRA Volunteers by the SAS after the IRA had opened fire on Coalisland RUC barracks, on February 16, 1992. The others were: Sean O'Farrell (23), Peter Clancy (20) and Daniel Vincent (20).

signatories of the Proclamation. It would be like talking about the Cuban Revolution and omitting the roles of Fidel Castro or Che Guevara. Or talking about the freedom struggle against apartheid in South Africa and leaving out Nelson Mandela. For a copy of the Proclamation *as Gaeilge* they used Google's translation tool which mangled the text. After widespread criticism they produced a second video which was even worse than the first. Not only did it exclude the names of the leaders of the 1916 Rising—as if they would contaminate today's youth—they included footage of unionist leader Ian Paisley, British Conservative Prime Minister David Cameron, the British queen, and such 'republican freedom fighters' as singers Bono of U2 and Bob Geldof, both holding honorary knighthoods of the British Empire.

Then there was the Justice Minister Charlie Flanagan's debacle in January 2020 when he proposed a commemorative service for the Royal Irish Constabulary and Dublin Metropolitan Police. Under its aegis, RIC constables and cadets, the Black and Tans and the Auxiliaries would also have been commemorated. That is, it would have morally equated those who gave their lives fighting for freedom with those who oppressed Irish people and enforced British rule. Could you imagine the reception if a call were made by some future Ukrainian cabinet minister to commemorate those Russian soldiers who died in the 2022 invasion and those Ukrainians who worked with them?

It was the RIC who had killed Sinn Féin Lord Mayor of Cork Thomas MacCurtain in March 1920, prior to the deployment of the notorious Black and Tans. After widespread opposition (including from Fianna Fáil members), the event was 'deferred'.

In 2020, RTÉ came under pressure for broadcasting the *Unquiet Graves* documentary about the Glenanne Gang, whose members included *serving* members of the Royal Ulster Constabulary police and British Army, and who killed over one hundred and twenty innocent civilians. Despite the documentary revealing the scale of collusion, the same Charlie Flanagan and commentators such as Eoghan Harris, in concert with the unionist daily *News Letter,* attempted to undermine the content with spurious questions about the funding of the film.

The prevailing and false narrative that kept successive Irish Governments complacent and from truly acting on behalf of the besieged nationalist community in the North was that the conflict was mainly IRA generated. Since the IRA called an end to its armed struggle, however, the past conflict has been more dispassionately explored. RTÉ's documentary was attacked because that false narrative is being upended. That collusion between British state forces and unionist death squads took place is now incontestable. Indeed, in the case of the killing of human rights lawyer Pat Finucane British Prime Minister David Cameron apologised for the killing and the collusion that had taken place. RUC officers had proposed to loyalists that he be killed, gave the information to his killers (who were all state agents), failed to stop the attack and then obstructed the murder investigation.

Landing of arms at Howth, July 1914

The Road to 1916

The 1916 Proclamation refers to several previous attempts to bring an end to British rule in Ireland and establish independence: 'In every generation the Irish people have asserted their right to national freedom and sovereignty; six times during the past three hundred years they have asserted it in arms.'

Those attempts had been under the banner of republicanism since the 1798 Rebellion by the United Irishmen. What gave added agency to the decision by, principally, the Irish Republican Brotherhood to launch the Rising was the failure of peaceful and constitutional efforts to achieve even a modicum of devolution, Home Rule (within the United Kingdom).

Home Rule (The Government of Ireland Act, 1914), technically on the statute book in 1914, had been resisted from the outset by Irish unionists. Unionist fear of the Catholic complexion of any future Home Rule central government in Dublin was certainly not groundless. The visceral fear of reprisal for the historical Plantation cannot also be underestimated. It was the loss of political and economic power, and the system of sectarian privilege that underpinned it, that more concerned the Protestant Ascendency. It had had no problem with a united Ireland as long as it was in control. Unionists opposed every extension of the franchise in the late nineteenth century, including reforms which increasingly saw local authorities across the country coming under the control of nationalists—apart from Belfast and seats of local government in the north-east.

The unionists wanted a continuation of the political relationship that guaranteed privilege and had emerged from the establishment of the United Kingdom after the dissolution of the Irish Parliament in 1800—that is integration, with MPs being returned to Westminster. Of course, after Catholic emancipation and the emergence of the Irish Parliamentary Party (IPP) as a force, the campaign for Home Rule began more earnestly and was considerably advanced when the IPP held the balance of power at Westminster. In the last election to be held on a restricted franchise before the outbreak of war, the IPP won seventy percent of the seats, the Irish Unionist Alliance under seventeen percent.

Unionist opposition came from its stronghold in northern counties in Ulster. Aided by conservative supporters in Britain, unionists formed an illegal private army, the Ulster Volunteer Force (UVF), which drilled and armed without official opposition. Amongst other politicians, they were encouraged by the leader of the Conservative Party, Andrew Bonar Law, who said, 'There are things stronger than parliamentary majorities . . . I can imagine no length of resistance to which Ulster will go which I shall not be ready to support', referring to illegality and armed rebellion.

In response, the Irish Volunteers were formed in 1913 to 'secure and maintain the rights and liberties common to the whole people of Ireland.' Among its membership and leadership were Irish republicans who had limited influence. Unlike in the North with UVF gunrunning, the Irish Volunteers were attacked by British forces after the landing of arms at Howth in 1914. The organisation, transport and landing of the republican arms was organised by anti-sectarian Protestant nationalists like Erskine Childers, Molly Childers, Mary Spring Rice and Conor O'Brien.[11]

---

[11] See *Rebel Prods: The Forgotten Story of Protestant Radical Nationalists and the 1916 Rising* by Valerie Jones

When WWI broke out, the Home Rule Act was suspended for the duration of the war—but with the absolute certainty that an Amending Bill would give unionists what they wanted before it became law. The British Prime Minister, Herbert Asquith, publicly pledged that 'employment of force, any kind of force, for what you call the coercion of Ulster is an absolutely unthinkable thing… [It] is a thing we would never countenance or consent to.'

During this period John Redmond, the incredibly inept, incompetent if not naïve leader of the IPP, made two fatal decisions.[12]

Firstly, he conceded that some counties in Ulster could opt out of Home Rule for a limited period. That fractured the integrity of Ireland as a political unit. In 1914 Lloyd

---

[12] On scores of occasions Redmond had pledged himself and his party to protecting the essential unity of Ireland, as in this speech in Limerick in October 1913: 'Irish Nationalists can never be assenting parties to the mutilation of the Irish nation; Ireland is a unit. It is true that within the bosom of a nation there is room for diversities of the treatment of government and of administration, but a unit Ireland is and Ireland must remain… The two-nation theory is to us an abomination and a blasphemy.'
Redmond fits Fine Gael's definition of the perfect statesman. Former Taoiseach John Bruton, decrying the number of statues to republican leaders, has called for a statue/bust in honour of Redmond, and boasted that he had secured from Britain 'the principle of legislative independence'—when he really means Redmond secured devolution for the Twenty-Six Counties.

George (British Prime Minister, 1916-22) told Redmond that the exclusion of four north-eastern counties would be strictly temporary and that they would be returned automatically after six years. Then, in talks in 1916, Lloyd George went on to include Tyrone and Fermanagh, which had nationalist majorities, bringing the number of excluded counties to six—again, allegedly, on a temporary basis during the emergency period of the war. However, in talks with Edward Carson, Lloyd George assured him that the exclusion of six counties was to be permanent.

Secondly, Redmond encouraged the Irish Volunteers to enlist in the British war effort—which split the organisation. Imagine thinking that by becoming a recruiting sergeant he would ingratiate the cause of Ireland with the British and they would subsequently reward us? For all his intentions of 'saving lives' and preventing bloodshed in the North Redmond's decisions resulted in the squander of thousands of Irish Volunteers' deaths at the Front. Pandering to Edward Carson and James Craig only emboldened them. The threats from the UVF, the Unionists, their Tory allies (and mutinous British Army officers) to set up a Provisional government for Ulster, to defy the democratic will of parliament certainly represented a British constitutional crisis. That should have been allowed to resolve itself once and for all. The alternative was only to stretch out the conflict for another century with the fatalities of the Tan War deaths, the pogroms against nationalists in 1920/21 in which hundreds lost their lives, and nationalists their homes and businesses, the Civil War, and the most recent conflict where thousands more people died.

The failure of the Irish Parliamentary Party to understand imperialism and colonialism, that party's flawed and damaging compromises, showed that its leaders were putty in the hands of the British.

A majority of the Irish Volunteers sided with Redmond, led to believe that in fighting for the freedom of small nations such as Belgium they were advancing and securing Irish claims to Home Rule. That huge disparity between those small numbers fighting for Ireland during the Rising and those fighting for Britain inspired Canon Charles O'Neill, the parish priest of Kilcoo, County Down, to include these bitter, haunting lyrics in his song *The Foggy Dew*:

> 'Twas far better to die 'neath an Irish sky
> Than at Suvla or Sud el Bar...
> 'Twas Britannia bade our Wild Geese go
> That small nations might be free
> But their lonely graves are by Sulva's waves
> Or the shore of the Great North Sea

Oh, had they died by Pearse's side
Or fought with Cathal Brugha
Their names we will keep where the fenians sleep
'Neath the shroud of the foggy dew

Irish people were not the only ones fooled by British promises. Ireland was not the only colony to supply Britain with military might. The cannon fodder came from all continents, all colonies, and they sacrificed themselves in all theatres of war without their sacrifices translating into freedom for their nations, big or small. In 1914, India was in a state of growing political unrest and the Indian National Congress was seeking independence. Encouraged to believe that the cause of independence, or at least self-government, would be served by fighting for Britain, Indians flocked to the war. But they too were badly let down. It was to be 1947 before India was granted independence (which included the partitioning of the subcontinent).[13]

---

[13] A British intelligence report from 1921 said that the IRA had plans to train Indian communists in guerrilla warfare. The IRA and Indian radicals in Britain also had ambitious plans to attack government buildings and police stations, destroy railway lines and telegraph communications 'to paralyse the Government in every way possible'. However, it is clear from the operations the IRA did carry out that it was severely limited in what it could do.

In the Middle East, in 1916, Britain promised the Arabs (including those in Palestine) 'complete and final liberation' if they would rise up against the Turks. After the war, Britain, with France, reneged on its pledges, drew borders here and there and partitioned the region regardless of the wishes of the local inhabitants.

The Palestinians are still waiting for their independence. Ronald Storrs, British governor of Jerusalem and Judea, said that the purpose of the Balfour Declaration was to form a 'little loyal Jewish Ulster in a sea of potentially hostile Arabism'.

The leaders of the Irish Republican Brotherhood had a better reading of the situation and of the imperialist mindset. While Carson's unionists and Redmond's nationalists were away at the Front, the Irish Republican Brotherhood, supported by James Connolly's Irish Citizen Army, struck at home. At Easter 1916, they declared a Republic, paying for it with their lives. Britain's betrayal of the estimated more than 35,000 Irish who died for the freedom of this small nation, and the threat to seek even more blood sacrifices through conscription to the British Army, undermined and destroyed Redmond's Parliamentary Party. It was supplanted by Sinn Féin in the 1918 general election, based on full male franchise for those over twenty-one and for women over twenty-seven. Britain's betrayal shattered and overshadowed the lives of returning war veterans who faced public apathy and animosity in a land experiencing a political revolution.

From the unionist point of view, their men (in the UVF's 36th Ulster Division) fought to prevent Home Rule and to maintain the union with Britain for all thirty-two counties or, failing that, for six of Ulster's nine counties. The 36th Ulster Division could take pride in their war. They had something to show for their suffering.

For unionists, the reality of a Catholic-Protestant, evenly-divided Ulster, temporarily opting out of Home Rule, didn't give them the monopoly on power which they wanted. The Ulster Unionist Party ditched its brethren in Donegal, Cavan and Monaghan in return for consolidating power over the Six Counties.

Mandate

The 1916 leaders and the republican volunteers who took up arms did not have an electoral mandate. The British, having refused to be moved by force of argument would be confronted with the argument of force. The republicans of 1916 had the powerful, simple, reality of experiencing life under British rule. The Irish Parliamentary Party had an electoral mandate, which they abused in recruiting for the war, but their MPs withdrew permanently from Westminster in early 1918.[14]

Being subjugated by Britain was increasingly intolerable, was regarded as illegitimate. Britain was, to paraphrase Wolfe Tone, 'the never-failing source of all our political evils'.

Justification for resistance in any colonial situation comes from the oppression a people or community experience directly. It is the choice of last resort. Not everyone will resist. Many within any community would have qualms about their own involvement in violence. Many would object perhaps to particular methods of violence, or doubt the efficacy of violence or whether the magnitude of deaths, pain and general suffering which would result would be

---

[14] The British government's attitude on the issue of mandates is informative. In 1972 when Gerry Adams had *no* electoral mandate the British released him from internment and flew him and other leaders of the Republican Movement by RAF aircraft to England for peace talks with government representatives. In 1982 when Gerry Adams *had* an electoral mandate the British Government refused to talk to Sinn Féin and introduced an Exclusion Order against Adams which meant he could be sentenced to five years in jail if he entered England to give a speech. The British government's mantra to the prisoners at the time of the 1981 hunger strike was, 'How can we talk to you, you have no mandate?' Bobby Sands' election, his becoming an MP, was an opportunity for compromise. Instead, Margaret Thatcher rushed through emergency legislation banning political prisoners like Sands from standing for election.

justified by or commensurate to their personal sense of grievance. Others will persuasively argue and give hope that change is possible through political action alone.

IRA activity during the Tan War was not ubiquitous. There were a large number of areas which did not physically participate in the struggle. A small percentage engaged in active resistance—enough to undermine British authority. A larger number engaged in passive resistance. Many put up no resistance of any kind and accommodated to the realities to conduct their daily lives.

In December 2020, Leo Varadkar said: 'There is a profound difference between the War of Independence fought then and the campaign of violence waged by the Provisional IRA in modern times. The War of Independence had democratic legitimacy.'

Varadkar completely ignores the fact that *before* the general election the IRA (as it was becoming known) was *preparing* for war.

The Volunteers were drilling, carrying out military manoeuvres, organising, preparing to renew resistance, and arming for guerrilla war well before the general election. The Volunteers had set up a GHQ, with Michael Collins (who was also the treasurer of the IRB) as adjutant general. Collins also organised with republicans in Britain the

'The constant glorification of past violence by Sinn Féin will only serve to make a united Ireland harder to achieve… and threatens the spirit of the Decade of Centenaries.' Leo Varadkar, December 2020.

importing of arms, gelignite, blasting powder and detonators for a renewed military struggle. It is simply not credible to rely on the 1918 election as a referendum approving the use of violence.

Fianna Fáil and Fine Gael claim that the 1916 Rising was retrospectively legitimised as a result of the post-war 1918 election, when Sinn Féin won 73 seats out of 105 and effectively eclipsed the Irish Parliamentary Party. By this logic, Sinn Féin overtaking the SDLP in 2001 amounts to retrospective justification for the IRA's armed struggle. That would be a farcical claim. But I do believe in the right to revolt whether as a majority, or an artificially-created minority, if there is no relief from intolerable political and socio-economic conditions and if the state relies upon repressive measures to function.

It is true that in its 1918 election manifesto Sinn Féin pledged to make 'use of any and every means available to render impotent the power of England to hold Ireland in subjection by military force or otherwise'. Perhaps the electorate understood exactly what that entailed. Perhaps not.

The historian Tomás Mac Conmara points out in his book *Days of Hunger* that an Irish Republican Brotherhood member, John Joe Neylon, laid claim to be the first republican to fire on the police since the Rising. In March 1917, Neylon wounded RIC Constable Johns by a shotgun blast. 'It put him out of action for a good while and he gave no more trouble after that,' said Neylon.

Had there been no general election in December 1918, or had the results for Sinn Féin been a less-decisive victory, the IRA would *still* have launched its campaign.

It was mere coincidence that two RIC policemen were killed at Soloheadbeg on the same day that Dáil Éireann opened on 21 January 1919. It was certainly not synchronised. IRA legend Dan Breen, who went on to become a Fianna Fáil TD, later said: 'We took the action deliberately, having thought over the matter and talked it over between us. [Seán] Treacy had stated to me that the only way of starting a war was to kill someone, and we wanted to start a war, so we intended to kill some of the police whom we looked upon as the foremost and most important branch of the enemy forces ... The only regret that we had following the ambush was that there were only two policemen in it, instead of the six we had expected.'

Neither the republicans nor Free Staters in their election manifestos sought a licence to fight a brutal and bloody civil war. The imposition of a treaty no side wanted, signed under the threat of renewed British violence on a massive scale, vitiated or at least certainly undermined the election as representing the free will of the people.

Those in Fine Gael who argue the democratic mandate of the Provisional Government ignore the fact that Free State forces attacked the Four Courts on June 28 before the convening of the 'Third Dáil', due on 1 July.

On 12 July, 1922, Michael Collins declared himself Commander in Chief of the pro-Treaty National Army and vested all power in an unconstitutional three-man War Council composed of himself, Richard Mulcahy and Eoin O'Duffy.

When Diarmuid Crowley, the Supreme Justice of the Dáil Courts ruled that anti-Treaty prisoners who had not been charged must be freed and that the Dáil must convene, Collins' government abolished the Court and imprisoned Crowley.

Meetings of the new legislative body were repeatedly prorogued. An anti-Treaty TD Laurence Ginnell from Longford-Westmeath, who attended the first session on 9 September 1922, challenged the legitimacy and authority of the government and demanded to know, 'Whether this is Dáil Éireann or a partition parliament... is this Dáil for the whole of Ireland?' He was then expelled.

This was how the Free State was born.

The Road to 1968

The British state of 'Northern Ireland' was imposed on the majority of people in Ireland. Northern nationalists were the main losers and victims. To say that it has never worked would be an understatement. It was enforced and upheld by violence and the ongoing threat of violent coercion. It is synonymous with violence. Had the monolithic Ulster Unionist Party tried to make nationalists/Catholics feel welcome they could have, but they didn't. If they had, the narrative might have been different.

Before and after the foundation of the state, there was a pogrom against Catholic areas in Belfast with five hundred killed, sixty percent of them Catholics, who were a minority in the city, between June 1920 and July 1922. My maternal grandparents were among the thousands driven from their homes. Thousands of Catholic males, including many World War One British

Army veterans, and a thousand women in the linen mills, along with 'rotten Protestants' (that is, socialists and progressives) were expelled from their jobs in Belfast and from their homes.

Throughout the Tan War, the IRA knew of the probability that there would be reprisals for its actions but reprisals never deterred it. And so places like Balbriggan and Cork were sacked and burned by British forces. Nationalist homes in Dromore and Banbridge in County Down came under attack in July 1920. They paid the price for the IRA killing of Banbridge native RIC Divisional Commander Gerald Smyth in Cork. In an infamous speech that provoked an RIC mutiny in Listowel, County Kerry, Smyth had urged, in effect, a policy of shoot first, ask no questions. Michael Collins ordered the killing of Detective Inspector Swanzy a month later for his role in the assassination of the Lord Mayor of Cork, Tomás Mac Curtain. Swanzy's assassination in Lisburn in August 1920 by the IRA led to Catholic shops and public houses being looted and burnt, the parochial house and an Ancient Order of Hibernians hall being set alight, and hundreds of Catholic families becoming refugees. By September, in the weaving and bleaching industries along the River Bann, five hundred Catholics workers were expelled.

Unionist supporters pose outside the burnt-out Catholic parochial house in Lisburn, 1920.

The history of sectarian clashes and violence against nationalists up until 1969 is comprehensively documented in *Holy War in Belfast,* by Andrew Boyd. Another publication, *Facts And Figures of the Belfast Pogrom, 1920-1922* was written by G. B. Kenna, a pseudonym for a Catholic priest, Fr John Hassan. This book was initially supported by the Free State administration but was then suppressed in case it increased sympathy for Northern nationalists and diverted Free State militarists from concentrating their energies against the IRA. 'It can have no effect but to make certain of our people see red, which will never do us any good,' said Ernest Blythe, Provisional Government, who also wanted nationalists to recognise the

Belfast Government and accept their lot.[15]

In his book, *A Treatise on Northern Ireland, Vol II*, Brendan O'Leary writes: 'In a foretaste of things to come, in October 1922, a Northern nationalist deputation arrived in Dublin, including priests, solicitors, and local councillors, looking for funds to counteract unionist propaganda. They got short shrift from Minister for Justice and External Affairs Kevin O'Higgins [echoing Blythe's actions in August]: "We have no other policy for the North East than we have for any other part of Ireland and that is the Treaty policy" … The washing of Southern hands could hardly have been more apparent.'[16]

The nationalist community had been extremely nervous about their fate since Redmond had effectively sold them out in principle—before his party had been eclipsed in 1918. But there were also concerns about the attitudes and ignorance of many in the national republican leadership, particularly those with little direct experience of unionists.

In his book *Northern Divisions,* the historian Jim McDermott writes:

'Sinn Féin in Belfast was not always happy with their leadership's views on the north. For the northern

---

[15] *Holy War in Belfast* by Andrew Boyd, Anvil Books, 1969.

[16] *A Treatise on Northern Ireland, Volume II: Control* by Brendan O'Leary, Oxford University Press, 2020.

membership of Sinn Féin, the prevention of partition was as important as the attainment of a republic. They were uneasy at the lack of priority given to this issue by the Dáil, and would have found general agreement with Louis B. Walshe, a Ballycastle solicitor and leading Sinn Féiner, who spoke at the 1919 Sinn Féin Ard Fheis in Dublin, urging that attention be given to Ulster, "for he thought the organisation had not sufficiently grappled with that question."

'The criticism was a valid one and was to be a continuing cause of concern to republicans in the north for the next three years. It is another reason why so many northern activists were drawn close to Michael Collins, who not only took a great interest in northern affairs, but who was at pains to keep in close contact with the Northern IRA leadership.'[17]

The IRA in Belfast and the Northern counties *before* partition enjoyed great support from GHQ in Dublin and could call upon huge resources and comradeship, such was national sentiment. During the Tan War, no distinction was drawn between an IRA attack on British soldiers in Crossmaglen and one in Crossbarry. Similarly, the IRA's defensive role in Derry and Belfast was acknowledged and

---

[17] *Northern Divisions—The Old IRA and the Belfast Pogroms 1920-22* by Jim McDermott, Beyond The Pale, 2001.

understood by the national leadership (including those who subsequently broke away to form Fianna Fáil in 1926). Thus, the IRA in Derry in 1920 and during the Belfast pogroms in 1920/21 is recognised as legitimate—but not in 1970/71 (for example, at the time of the 'Battle of St Matthews' in Ballymacarret when the British Army left the area defenceless).[18]

'Our violence was good, yours bad.'

In the January 1920 municipal elections, a nationalist majority was returned in Derry. When partition was mooted, the nationalist community in the city expected that they would be included, along with Donegal, in the 'Southern area'. In June 1920, the unionist Ulster Volunteer Force in the Fountain area of Derry opened fire on nationalist Bishop Street, killing three civilians. Guns from Donegal were sent to the IRA and in gun battles another seventeen people lost their lives. These included a ten-year-

---

[18] On 27 June 1970 trouble broke out across Belfast after Orange parades. In East Belfast as an Orange lodge and band paraded past St Matthew's Catholic Church on the Newtownards Road their supporters attacked the small Catholic enclave of Ballymacarret/Short Strand with petrol bombs, setting fire to the home of the sexton and his family and to a Catholic bar. The Catholic residents appealed to the British Army to intervene but they claimed they were overstretched. IRA Volunteers took up a defensive position in the grounds of St Matthew's and in a gun battle which lasted several hours repelled the attack, and saved the chapel and nearby homes. Three people were killed: two Protestant men, Robert Neill and Robert McCurrie, and one of the defenders of St Matthew's, Henry McIlhone.

old orphan, George Caldwell, and Howard McKay, the son
of the governor of the unionist Apprentice Boys, who was
placed up against a wall and summarily shot dead by
republicans. Once unionists were in power they
gerrymandered electoral boundaries. It gave the unionist
minority permanent control of the council for the next fifty
years.

After partition, the nationalist community was
overwhelmingly outgunned. The Civil War in the Free State
compounded its sense of desolation, isolation and
demoralisation.

The Boundary Commission

Free State representatives and pro-Treaty supporters in
debates and in the media had hawked the Boundary
Commission as a stepping stone to freedom and that the
Council of Ireland (consisting of representatives from North
and South) would facilitate unity. But it was deceptive
thinking on their part if they thought that the Commission
(with its built-in British and Unionist majority) would
adjust the border.

'Since the ratification of the Treaty,' observed Michael
Farrell in his authoritative work, *The Orange State*, 'Collins
seemed to accept partition as irrevocable, relying on the

Boundary Commission to transfer the bulk of the North's Catholics to the South, and hoping to negotiate better conditions for the rest.' Unionist leader Sir James Craig (now prime minister in the North) stated that he would never give in to any rearrangement of the boundary. In other words, 'Not an inch', 'What we have, we hold.'[19]

When the London *Morning Post* leaked the draft Commission report and coloured maps of the border in November 1925, revealing that not only would Derry City, Fermanagh and Tyrone *not* be transferred to the South but that parts of Donegal would be transferred to the North, Free State representatives rushed to London to have the report suppressed—it was only declassified in 1968 and published in 1969. In the words of W.T. Cosgrave, the report should be 'burned or buried'. The Free Staters were desperate and needed a fig leaf to cover the incompetence of the strategy they had proclaimed. They now appealed to the British Government to reconsider the onerous terms of the financial reparations demanded of them otherwise their 'political existence' was in doubt. Sir James Craig accused them of having lived 'in a fool's paradise' if they thought the Commission would deliver unity.

---

[19] *The Orange State* by Michael Farrell, Pluto Press, 1976.

In return for accepting partition and its fixed border the Free State was given relief from paying off its 'share' of UK public debt but it was to continue to pay the pensions to ex-RIC officers and agreed to pay compensation awards for war damage caused since 1919.

The minutes of the British cabinet meeting held on 2 December 1925, which included Churchill, Birkenhead and Balfour, are damning. They were discussing the meeting they had just held with the Free State representatives and Craig.

The minutes noted that the 'Irish Free State … were making no further claims upon Sir James Craig in regard to the treatment of Roman Catholics and other internal affairs in Northern Ireland.'

In addition, a personal understanding had been arrived at between Sir James Craig and the Irish Free State representatives for more friendly co-operation, but this could not be put in writing. The Irish Free State, however, were making no further claims upon Sir James Craig in regard to the treatment of Roman Catholics and other internal affairs in Northern Ireland.

Bad enough that northern nationalists had been officially abandoned by the Free State, but its successive leaders had the hubris to subsequently lecture the nationalist community on how it should and shouldn't respond to its oppression. Meantime Fianna Fáil mythologised, exploited and glorified the Good Old IRA, with Fine Gael in particular engaging in hagiography when it came to Michael Collins, 'the man who fought the Black and Tan terror until England was forced to offer terms.'

If Michael Collins had had access to the weaponry of the modern IRA is anyone suggesting he would not have deployed it?

Would Collins have used Semtex, had it been available?

Guerrilla organisations tend to be decentralised to allow activists to use their own initiative, improvise and carry out opportunistic attacks. This flexibility, however, comes at a cost in control and direction, with the political and military leadership having to accept and share in responsibility for disastrous operations. Dáil Éireann (1919-1922), despite Sinn Féin and IRA dual memberships in many cases, did not exercise overall authority of the IRA.

One cannot single out and take pride in the heroism of all the purely military operations on the one hand and, on the other hand, wring your hands at the large-scale shooting of informers, the large number of disappearances, or the deaths of civilians during IRA raids on houses. The same Volunteers carried out 'good' and 'bad' operations, and whatever measure of independence the Southern state has today it owes to the bloody, net effect of the IRA's armed struggle and the sacrifices of its Volunteers and supporters, which was waged to achieve national independence.

A diminished IRA remained organised in the North but its position was desperate. Objectively, it was never in a position to overturn the state. It lacked the potency of a united independence struggle which had at one time translated into negotiating muscle but which had been compromised and frittered away by the 1921 Anglo-Irish Treaty, which complemented partition. The IRA's activities in the North prior to 1970, including the failed, mainly Southern-led Border Campaign (1956-62), did not amount to an existential threat to the state.

What the IRA did maintain was an organisational structure and also a tradition of struggle, around which there was a political and cultural subculture, and a long litany of prison experience. Throughout the history of the Northern state there was one two-year period in the early 1950s when there were no political prisoners. When I was interned in 1972 it was with older republicans who had been in jail in the 1940s, and they in the 1940s had been imprisoned with republicans who had been interned in the 1920s, by the British or Free Staters. We felt part of a living tradition of struggle with roots in the past, linking us to 1916 and beyond.

The Ulster Unionist Government used wide-ranging repressive laws, including the Special Powers Act, allowing for summary detention with no access to a solicitor, suspension of habeas corpus, internment, punishment by flogging, the banning of inquests, the banning of meetings, prohibiting the circulation of any newspaper, prohibiting the possession of any film or gramophone record, the destruction of any building, and arrest for the spreading by word of mouth or text any 'reports or ... statements intended or likely to cause disaffection to subjects of His Majesty.' Section 15 also allowed the Minister for Home Affairs to create new crimes by decree (thus, in the 1960s, the Minister made it a crime to name a club a Republican Club). It would crush not just any sign of resistance but was hostile to all aspects of nationalism, from Gaelic Athletic Association sports to the Irish language. This was even reflected in the content of what the local BBC broadcast, expending, for example, huge resources on its annual *Mardi Gras*-like coverage of the Orange Order marching season.

For all intents and purposes, nationalists didn't count.[20]

As if the Special Powers Act hadn't given it enough power, the Unionist Government in 1954 then introduced the Flags and Emblems Act. It became an offence to interfere

---

[20] As a child I remember republicans being pointed out in the street with an attitude of awe and respect as someone who had served time in England or who had been flogged for his political beliefs. One such man was Pat McCotter. Others who suffered that painful and humiliating punishment included Ned Tennyson (Portadown), Jimmy Greenway (Lurgan), Albert O'Rawe (Belfast), Patrick McGuigan (Belfast), and Pat Donnelly and John McMahon (both, Armagh).
'Two instruments were used to inflict the punishment: the cat o' nine tails for those aged over eighteen and the birch for those under that age. The whip was applied to the bared upper back, the offender being strapped to an apparatus. Those who were birched were made to bend over and the instrument was used on their bare buttocks. The whip inflicted by far the heavier punishment.' - *Irish Political Prisoners 1920-1962* by Sean McConville. McConville also quotes from an account given by Liam Burke, OC of A Wing, Crumlin Road Prison, which appears in Uinseann MacEoin's book, *The IRA in the Twilight Years*. Burke refers to James Meaney, Joe Doyle and Arthur Steele who had been sentenced to twelve years penal servitude and twelve strokes of the cat.
'On a cold night close to Christmas preparations for the punishments began. The men were taken from their own cell to an empty cell in C Wing and were locked in, together with the prison staff. They were ordered to strip off their shirts and to await their turn for the punishment. Each was eventually escorted through ranks of watching officers to the boiler house. There they were suspended by rings, hands and feet, inches above the ground. A hooded prison officer then administered the whipping or birching. Each stroke was counted off by the Governor while the prison medical officer checked the men's heart. After punishment, the man was taken down and escorted back to his cell, the only treatment being a gauze bandage over the bleeding parts.'

with the flying of the Union flag, the 'Union Jack', and effectively made it an offence to fly the Irish Tricolour—on the grounds that it was likely to cause a breach of the peace. During the 1964 general election, at the behest of the Reverend Ian Paisley, the Royal Ulster Constabulary, using pickaxes and iron bars, smashed their way into the campaign office of republican candidate Billy McMillan at 145 Divis Street in west Belfast to seize the Tricolour, provoking six nights of rioting and protests. Because Sinn Féin was proscribed, McMillan ran under the banner of 'The Republican Party'. Hundreds were injured in baton charges and scores of people, including a mother of eight, were arrested and subsequently imprisoned for up to six months. [21]

In the first years of the Northern state, nationalist elected representatives abstained from the Belfast parliament. Later they took their seats in Stormont, their numbers depleted by the unionists having abrogated one of the protections of the Government of Ireland Act, elections by proportional representation.

---

[21] It is interesting to look at the names of some of those charged. For example, a young married man, 22-year-old Brian Keenan, later ends up in the ranks of the IRA and becomes its Chief of Staff. Others are among those rounded up and interned in Long Kesh in 1971.

For fifty years, nationalist representatives had no say in or influence over social and economic policy, housing, employment, the location of industries, health, services, transport, or the budget. As has often been wryly cited, in fifty years only one nationalist-sponsored legislative bill was successfully introduced—the Wild Birds Protection Act, in 1931. When its elected representatives went into parliament and engaged with the Ulster Unionist Party they were ignored, humiliated and treated contemptuously.

Two civil rights pamphlets, *Eye-Witness in Northern Ireland* (1968) and *Northern Ireland: The Plain Truth* (1969), outlined shocking statistics on the gerrymandering of electoral wards to produce unionist-dominated councils where nationalists were either in the majority or where the population was evenly balanced. The franchise was restricted to 'householders and their wives', that is, ratepayers. Because of the low number of houses in nationalist areas, there was massive overcrowding with thousands of Catholics of voting age not qualifying for the register: the pamphlets estimate that it affected a quarter of a million voters. But shopkeepers and business owners, the majority of whom were unionist, received extra votes for their premises. (Thus the civil rights demand of 'One Man, One Vote.')

Stormont also deliberately neglected to invest west of the River Bann (which roughly bisects the North) in the three counties of Derry, Tyrone and Fermanagh, favouring instead Antrim, Down and north Armagh, predominantly unionist. An official report in 1969 showed fifteen investments in industries west of the Bann compared to fifty-nine in the east. This discrimination was also evident when Stormont refused to upgrade Derry's Magee College to university status and instead built a new university in the unionist town of Coleraine.

Depriving nationalists of houses, jobs or prospects resulted in emigration, with nationalists disproportionally making up over sixty percent of those who left. Even in 1960, the majority of children in the North were Catholic, effectively nationalist. This did not translate into a nationalist majority because of higher Catholic emigration. In this way, the Unionist Party perpetuated its electoral supremacy. In Fermanagh, forty percent of nationalists in the 15- to 25-year-old bracket emigrated; the unionist figure seventeen percent. In Tyrone, the figures are thirty-five percent to eighteen percent. Ironically, from 1970, many weapons sent to the IRA, particularly from North America, were from those who felt they had been forced out by Stormont and its policies. The strong Irish-American community goes back further and is a product of British policy during and after the Famine. Indeed, US President Joe Biden referred to it at a press conference in March 2021. He said: 'When my great-grandfather got into a coffin ship in the Irish sea, expectation was, was he going to live long enough on that ship to get to the United States of America? But they left because of what the Brits had been doing,' he said. 'They were in real trouble, they didn't want to leave, but they had no choice,' he added.

Each pamphlet is replete with examples and statistics too detailed to reproduce but they irrefutably illustrate the link between gerrymandering, housing and employment.

Gerrymandering in Omagh: a nationalist population of over sixty-one percent gets to elect nine councillors; the unionist minority, twelve. The two unionist wards are small, the nationalist vote is contained in one large ward, the West Ward. Even if houses were built in the West Ward, the balance of power would never change as the number of council seats were restricted to nine.

'Catholics may be on housing waiting lists for up to twelve years or longer, whilst Protestants can often choose their council house and have it allocated before they are married,' notes *Voting Injustices, The Plain Truth* (The Campaign for Social Justice). This practice is replicated in Derry, Dungannon, Armagh, Enniskillen, Magherafelt, etc., and was eventually challenged in a civil rights action in Caledon by the occupation of a house (involving the mother, aunt and grandmother of Michelle Gildernew, later elected Sinn Féin MP for Fermanagh & South Tyrone).

The ramifications of unionists controlling what democratically should be a nationalist council then results in the following: only four nationalists employed among the Omagh County Hall staff of one hundred; only two nationalists employed as education officers among a staff of seventy; only two nationalists employed in rural council affairs out of a staff of thirty-five.

Through their rates nationalists were paying for their own discrimination.

And so on and so forth, right up to government public

bodies across the North. It runs through everything—education boards, post office staff, clerical staff, the hospitals authority, the government health service, appointments of chief medical officer, deputy chief, medical referees, county chief dental officer. Out of 390 hospital specialists, thirty-one were Catholic. Management committees of hospitals were made up of 456 members but only seventy-two were from a Catholic/nationalist background. Of sixteen public health inspectors, just three were Catholic. Out of eight Crown solicitors, not one was a Catholic. Out of fifty-three school inspectors, five were Catholic. The Post Office never had a Catholic director. Thirteen head post masters—no Catholic.

A huge pattern of sectarian employment policies was replicated in Belfast's main industries—shipbuilding, textiles and engineering. Male unemployment in places like Ballymurphy reached fifty percent.

It was impossible for a nationalist to identify with or have a stake in the Six-County state. Nationalists and republicans attempted to more aggressively change things through the Civil Rights Movement, plans for which were made in 1966 at the home of solicitor Kevin Agnew—my election agent in Mid-Ulster in 1983 and a member of Sinn Féin.

A Culture of Sectarian Discrimination

'A man in Fintona asked him how it was that he had over fifty percent Roman Catholics in his ministry. He thought that was too funny. He had one hundred and nine of a staff and, so far as he knew, there were four Roman Catholics. Three of these were civil servants, turned over to him whom he had to take when he began.'

Sir Edward Archdale, Unionist Minister of Agriculture, *Northern Whig*, 2 April 1925

'Another allegation made against the Government, and which was untrue, was that, of thirty-one porters at Stormont, twenty-eight were Roman Catholics. I have investigated the matter and I find that there are thirty Protestants, and only one Roman Catholic there temporarily.'

J. M. Andrews, Unionist Minister for Labour, 1933

'There was a great number of Protestants and Orangemen who employed Roman Catholics. He felt he could speak freely on this subject as he had not a Roman Catholic about his own place [Cheers]. He appreciated the great difficulty experienced by some of them in procuring suitable Protestant labour, but he would point out that the Roman Catholics were endeavouring to get in everywhere and were out with all their force and might to destroy the power and constitution of Ulster... He would appeal to loyalists, therefore, wherever possible to employ good Protestant lads and lassies.'

Sir Basil Brooke, junior government whip, 12 July 1933 (and, later, Stormont Prime Minister), *Fermanagh Times*, 13 July 1933

'When I made that declaration last 'Twelfth', I did so after careful consideration. What I said was justified. I recommended people not to employ Roman Catholics, who were ninety-nine percent disloyal.'

Sir Basil Brooke, *News Letter,* 20 March 1934

'The Hon. Member for South Fermanagh [Mr Healy] has raised the question of what is the Government's policy [in relation to the employment of Catholics]. My right Hon. Friend [Sir Basil Brooke] spoke [on 12 July 1933 and 19 March 1934] as a Member of His Majesty's Government. He spoke entirely on his own when he made the speech to which the Hon. Member refers, but there is not one of my colleagues who does not entirely agree with him, and I would not ask him to withdraw one word he said.'

Sir James Craig, Prime Minister, speaking on 20 March 1934

'I suppose I am about as high up in the Orange Institution as anybody else. I am very proud indeed to be Grand Master of the loyal County of Down. I have filled that office many years, and I prize that far more than I do being Prime Minister. I have always said I am an Orangeman first and a politician and Member of this Parliament afterwards... The Hon. Member must remember that in the South they boasted of a Catholic state. They still boast of Southern Ireland being a Catholic state. All I boast is that we are a Protestant Parliament and Protestant state.'

Sir James Craig, 1934, during a bitter debate on how the rights of nationalists had deteriorated since 1921

'There are ways of discovering whether a man is heart and soul in carrying out the intention of the Act of 1920, which was given to the Ulster people in order to save them from being swallowed up in a Dublin Parliament. Therefore, it is undoubtedly our duty and our privilege, and always will be, to see that those appointed by us possess the most unimpeachable loyalty to the King and Constitution. That is my whole object in carrying on a Protestant Government for a Protestant people. I repeat it in this House.'

Sir James Craig, Stormont Prime Minister, November 1934

'At a meeting in Derry to select candidates for the Corporation, Mr H. McLaughlin said that for the past forty-eight years since the foundation of his firm there had been only one Roman Catholic employed, and that was a case of mistaken identity.'

Mr H. McLaughlin, Ulster Unionist Party, September 1946, *Derry People*

'The nationalist majority in the county, i.e., Fermanagh, notwithstanding a reduction of 336 in the year, stands at 3,684. We must ultimately reduce and liquidate that majority. This county, I think it can be safely said, is a unionist county. The atmosphere is unionist. The boards and properties are nearly all controlled by unionists. But there is still this millstone [the nationalist majority] around our necks.'

E. C. Ferguson, Stormont MP, Ulster Unionist Party, 13 April 1948, *Irish News*

'He [Alex Hunter, Stormont MP] had been recently horrified to learn that a local authority within the combined Orange district had appointed a Roman Catholic to represent them in the County Antrim Education Committee.'

Northern Whig, July 13 1956

'You people of the Shankill Road, what's wrong with you? Number 425 Shankill Road—do you know who lives there? Pope's men, that's who! Fortes ice-cream shop, Italian Papists on the Shankill Road! How about 56 Aden Street? For ninety-seven years a Protestant lived in that house and now there's a Papisher in it. Crimea Street, number 38! Twenty-five years that house has been up, twenty-four years a Protestant lived there but there's a Papisher there now.'

Reverend Ian Paisley, addressing a rally in the lower Shankill, Belfast, June 1959

'Ulster has only room for one party.'

Basil Brooke, 1961

'We are not going to build houses in the South Ward and cut a rod to beat ourselves later on. We are going to see that the right people are put into these houses and we are not making any apology for it.'

Alderman George Elliot, speaking in Enniskillen, *Impartial Reporter*, 14 November 1963

'When it is remembered that the first Minister [for Home Affairs], Sir Dawson Bates, held that post for twenty-two years and had such a prejudice against Catholics that he made it clear to his Permanent Secretary that he did not want his most juvenile clerk, or typist, if a Papist, assigned for duty to his Ministry, what could one expect when it came to filling posts in the Judiciary, Clerkships of the Crown and Peace and Crown Solicitors?'

Mr G. C. Duggan, Northern Ireland Comptroller and Auditor-General, *Irish Times*, 4 May 1967

'It is frightfully hard to explain to Protestants that if you give Roman Catholics a good job and a good house they will live like Protestants because they will see neighbours with cars and television sets; they will refuse to have eighteen children. But if a Roman Catholic is jobless, and lives in the most ghastly hovel, he will rear eighteen children on National Assistance. If you treat Roman Catholics with due consider and kindness, they will live like Protestants in spite of the authoritative nature of their Church.'

Captain Terence O'Neill, Stormont Prime Minister, *Belfast Telegraph*, 10 May 1969

'We are satisfied that all these unionist-controlled councils have used and use their power to make appointments in a way which benefited Protestants. In the figures available for October 1968 only thirty percent of Londonderry Corporation's administrative, clerical and technical employees were Catholics. Out of the ten best-paid posts, only one was held by a Catholic. In Dungannon Urban District, none of the Council's administrative, clerical and technical employees was a Catholic. In County Fermanagh, no senior council posts (and relatively few others) were held by Catholics: this was rationalised by reference to 'proven loyalty' as a necessary test for local authority appointments. In that county, among about seventy-five drivers of school buses, at most seven were Catholics. This would appear to be a very clear case of sectarian and political discrimination.'

Cameron Report, Disturbances in Northern Ireland, 1969

'We must build up the dossiers on the men and women who are a menace to this country, because one day, ladies and gentlemen, if the politicians fail, it will be our duty to liquidate the enemy.'

Former Minister of Home Affairs, William Craig, addressing a Vanguard rally in Belfast's Ormeau Park, March 1972

'We are prepared to come out and shoot and kill. I am prepared to come out and shoot and kill, let's put the bluff aside. I am prepared to kill, and those behind me will have my full support.'

William Craig addressing the Conservative Monday Club in October 1972. Vanguard became the Vanguard Unionist Progressive Party and in 1974 Craig and two other members were elected to Westminster. In 1977 Britain appointed William Craig to the Council of Europe with, incredibly, a brief to report on human rights legislation. Despite his advocacy of violence RTÉ continued to interview Craig. He was never subject to Section 31

'... force means death and fighting, and whoever gets in our way, whether republicans or those sent by the British Government, there would be killings.'

John Taylor, addressing a Vanguard rally in Tobermore, October 1972

'If I was in control of this country, it would not be in the same state it is in now. I would cut off all supplies, including water and electricity, to Catholic areas. And I would stop Catholics from getting social security. It is the only way to deal with enemies of the state and to stamp out the present troubles.'

Charles Poots, DUP Councillor, North Down, 1975 (father of Edwin Poots, former DUP leader)

'One out of every three Roman Catholics one meets is either a supporter of murder or, worse still, a murderer.'

John Taylor, Ulster Unionist MP (later Lord Kilclooney), 1991

Catholics who objected to the singing of the British national anthem 'are just Fenian scum who have been indoctrinated by the Catholic Church. Taxpayers' money would be better spent on an incinerator and burning the lot of them. Their priests should be thrown in and burnt as well.'

DUP Councillor George Seawright at a meeting of the Belfast Education and Library Board, 1984. He was subsequently expelled from the DUP. Seawright was also a member of the Ulster Volunteer Force. He was assassinated by a republican splinter group, the Irish People's Liberation Organisation, in 1987

'As far as democratic politics is concerned, it's perfectly obvious Sinn Féin are not quite house-trained yet.'

Ulster Unionist Party leader David Trimble in 2000, using a dog metaphor when referring to republicans

'We do business with you because it is in the interest of Northern Ireland that we have peace in Northern Ireland. We hold our noses and do business with you.'

Edwin Poots, DUP MLA, 2015

'If anybody knows me, and indeed knows the Democratic Unionist Party, they know that I'm not going to put at risk to the people of Northern Ireland the possibility that rogue Sinn Féin or renegade SDLP ministers are going to take decisions that will harm the community in Northern Ireland.'

Arlene Foster, DUP leader 2015, when temporarily taking over the role of First Minister

Imagine if Cumann na nGaedheal had began redrawing constituencies which disenfranchised the voters of Fianna Fáil; refused to build houses or locate industries in areas where Fianna Fáil had support; marched through those areas every year, not on 12 July but on 30 May (the date of de Valera's 'dump arms' order) to crow about their defeat of republicans; and that this continued for fifty years. Would Fianna Fáil supporters meekly accept it? And, in this scenario, when they could take no more and marched for civil rights and for an end to discrimination, the Gardaí and Blueshirt gangs would baton them, shoot them, then burn thousands of them out of their homes to put manners on them.

In fact, when in the 1930s the first leaders of Fine Gael and the Blueshirts used violence and threatened a fascist takeover, Fianna Fáil members and the IRA fought back. One Fine Gael member, John L. Sullivan was convicted of attempting to burn down the home of a Fianna Fáil TD. He fought the local elections in 1936 from, as he put it, 'the Glasshouse in the Curragh'. He was finally elected a Fine Gael TD in the infamous 1973-77 Fine Gael/Labour coalition government.[22]

---

[22] The former British Army Curragh Camp was converted into a prison by the Free State. There, in December 1922 seven republicans were executed. Prisoners referred to the former barracks as 'The Glasshouse', because it had a distinctive glass roof.

The Road to 1969

When I moved down to the Iveagh/Broadway area from Andersonstown in west Belfast as a ten-year-old, the Orange Order still marched on the Falls Road every July. We just stood there, subdued, humiliated, reminded of our place in society, vanquished as the band played *God Save the Queen* before they processed into Broadway Presbyterian Church. By the same token, we weren't even allowed to parade into town to celebrate St Patrick's Day. We weren't allowed beyond Divis Street—and that remained the case until the peace process.

In 1966, the Republic of Ireland celebrated the fiftieth anniversary of the 1916 Rising with great pageantry. Plans were made by nationalists in Belfast to do the same. Belfast Corporation banned a Republican Party booking of the Ulster Hall for a concert to mark the anniversary. On the day of the parade through West Belfast, Stormont banned trains carrying republican supporters from Dublin and the Royal Ulster Constabulary set up police checkpoints along the Border to inhibit people travelling to the march.

Our community was to pay dearly for that commemoration.

A new unionist paramilitary organisation, calling itself the Ulster Volunteer Force, issued a statement saying that 'known IRA men will be executed mercilessly and without hesitation'. The Reverend Ian Paisley was associated with his own group, the Ulster Protestant Volunteers. The UVF killed three civilians. In an arson attack aimed at a Catholic-owned bar, they missed their intended target and as a result a seventy-seven-year-old Protestant woman, Matilda Goud, died from her burns. In a gun attack on the Falls Road, they killed John Scullion. In another gun attack, they shot dead eighteen-year-old Peter Ward from Beechmount. I remember watching his funeral as a thirteen-year-old and feeling bewildered—and frightened.

At fifteen, I was too young to travel to the civil rights march in Derry on 5 October 1968, but an older friend, Martin Taylor, was there and he described the RUC attack on marchers in Duke Street. I also watched on television three

Northern Ireland Civil Rights ASSOCIATION

A CIVIL RIGHTS MARCH

WILL BE HELD IN DERRY ON SATURDAY, 5TH OCT.

COMMENCING AT 3-30 p.m.

ASSEMBLY POINT: WATERSIDE RAILWAY STATION
MARCH TO THE DIAMOND
Where a PUBLIC METTING will take place

months later the scenes of People's Democracy students being attacked by unionists at Burntollet while their RUC collaborators stood by.

Throughout 1969 there were bomb attacks on electricity pylons and reservoirs. The IRA was blamed but later it emerged that unionists, including close acquaintances of Reverend Ian Paisley, were responsible. They were hoping to bring down Stormont Prime Minister, Terence O'Neill, a unionist who was otherwise under pressure to introduce reforms. They succeeded. He was replaced by the more hard line Major Chichester-Clark.

Paisley had set up his own church, the Free Presbyterian Church, his own sectarian newspaper, *The Protestant Telegraph*, which railed against Popery and 'Roman Catholics', and eventually his own party, the Protestant Unionist Party, which became the Democratic Unionist Party in 1971. It was more extreme than the Ulster Unionists, accusing them of selling out 'Ulster'. His apocalyptic sectarianism had popular support. He also established two paramilitary groups, The Third Force, and Ulster Resistance (involved in gun-running with the help of British Intelligence).

Besides talking about girls, dances and pop music, our conversation at school increasingly turned to politics. 'What was going on,' we wondered. (Out of our O-Level class of twenty-eight in 1969, five of us would end up interned in Long Kesh.)

Trouble broke out in Derry after a unionist Apprentice Boys parade in August. After several days of fighting in what became famous as 'The Battle of the Bogside', the RUC were exhausted. Stormont announced it was mobilising the B-

Specials reserves and sending in more police. The Civil Rights Association called for protests to be mounted in nationalist areas, the objective being to tie down the RUC and prevent reinforcements being sent to Derry. I went to the protest outside Hastings Street RUC Barracks in Divis Street but left for home, about two miles up the road, around 10 pm. Shortly afterwards, an invasion from the Shankill area began. Loyalists, B-Specials and the RUC invaded the Falls and burned down hundreds of houses. The sound of the gunfire throughout the night was terrifying.

When my friends and I went down the road the following morning, the scenes of smouldering houses and burnt-out buildings was apocalyptic. Snipers were still firing the odd shot down towards the Falls. Travellers with their lorries were helping people load whatever sticks of furniture they could retrieve from the smoking ruins. My friend Joe Doyle and his parents had escaped the unionist mob in their nightclothes, their house at 11 Conway Street and all their possessions, every memento and photograph, totally destroyed. At Divis Flats, we heard of two deaths, including that of a child, when the RUC sprayed thirteen homes with heavy machine-gun fire. A Herculean effort was being made to rip up paving stones and build barricades at every street corner. We went home and did the same with other men from our district, sealing off the five streets into Iveagh.

Those young people who joined the IRA in the North post-1969 did so, in the main, because they felt there was no one else to defend their homes and their areas. They could not rely on Taoiseach Jack Lynch and the Irish Government. They could not rely on the police, given that RUC armoured cars and machine-guns, and the B-Specials, had cleared the way for the arsonist mobs.

Despite all the warning signs that the Stormont Government and its supporters would go to extreme lengths to quell the civil rights movement, the IRA leadership failed to produce the arms to adequately defend nationalist areas in August 1969. I remember seeing the slogan, 'IRA = I Ran Away', painted on a Falls Road wall and it certainly expressed a sentiment shared by many. That failure was to contribute to a republican split a few months later. It also, ironically, led many nationalists to welcome the old enemy, the British Army, as defenders.

I recall when we were making sandwiches for soldiers based in Broadway Primary School in Iveagh Street, a republican, Stoker Cosgrove, telling us we were mad and would rue the day we hosted them. Two weeks later,

following three consecutive nights of rabble-rousing
speeches by Ian Paisley in the nearby Village area, unionists
looted Roddy's Bar and then, after midnight, attempted to
invade our area. We rushed out to defend the district. A
motorist was dragged from his car by the mob and when we
tried to go to his aid the soldiers turned their bayonets on
us. Scuffles broke out and there were several injuries.[23]

One of my neighbours, Jimmy Dempsey, collapsed
minutes after he got home from the melee and died. A
month after the attempted incursion into Iveagh, more
Catholics were burnt out of their homes in Coates Street,
behind Hastings Street Barracks, while the British Army
refused to intervene.

What concerned us teenagers in 1969 was the immediate
and terrible reality that our homes were being razed to the

---

[23] Stoker Cosgrove's son, Tommy, my age, would be interned twice for
four years in Long Kesh and later was on the H-Block blanket protest.
Stoker's daughter, Nora McCabe, a married mother of three, was killed
by a plastic bullet fired at her head by an RUC officer during the 1981
hunger strike when she went to her corner shop, yards from her home,
to buy a packet of cigarettes. The RUC denied having shot her. At the
inquest, two local women gave evidence, and film from a Canadian
camera crew indisputably showed the shot being fired from a jeep and
that there was no rioting in the area, as police claimed. RUC men
stormed out of the court. The RUC would not identify who fired the
shot. The DPP directed that no charges be brought. The officer who
gave the order to shoot Nora, Chief Superintendent Jimmy Crutchley,
was later promoted to Assistant Chief Constable and was mentioned in
the British Queen's Honour List.

ground, our relatives and friends were being killed, and it was all *legal* and there was no one prepared to help us— except for republican supporters in the South.

We had set out for civil rights, not for rebellion or revolution, and this was the lethal response of the Ulster Unionist Party Government at Stormont. No Ulster Unionist Party politician has ever been held to account. I don't know of anyone in that party who has even publicly questioned unionist behaviour.

Not one member of the RUC police was arrested, questioned or charged over the fatal beating to death of Sammy Devenney in front of his nine children in their Bogside home; for the fatal baton blow to the head of sixty-seven-year-old Francis McCloskey in Dungiven; for the killing of nine-year-old Patrick Rooney in his bed in Divis Flats; or for the first killing of a British soldier during the conflict, Trooper Hugh McCabe, home on leave, shot dead by the RUC whilst he tried to defend the people of the Falls. No member of the B-Specials (which a few months later would be reconstituted as the Ulster Defence Regiment, the UDR, a full regiment in the British Army) was arrested for shooting dead John Gallagher in Armagh, following a civil rights meeting.

None of these killings are or were referred to as violence by the Stormont Government, the British Government or the media. Between 1968 and 1970, the period before the IRA became active, most of the violence on the streets was either carried out by the state or unionists in support of the state.

In the pages of the *Belfast Telegraph* and *The News Letter* daily newspapers of that time you will not find an editorial condemning violence or a government minister being asked to condemn violence. In fact, you cannot even find the word 'condemn'. Rather, both papers use the word 'deplore' when giving their opinions on the activities of the Civil Rights Association. In early August 1969, *before* the Belfast pogroms, and *after* at least three Catholic civilians have already been killed by the RUC, an editorial in the *Belfast Telegraph* says, 'There is little to be gained by apportioning blame.'

'Violence' only begins when the IRA fires its first shot. After that, British soldiers 'kill' people, whereas the IRA 'murder'. By omitting or distorting and finessing the sequence of events of who *began* the violence, the British establishment, the unionist parties and much of the media manufactured a perception that the IRA was responsible. The IRA certainly becomes responsible thereafter and must bear responsibility for major horrific acts where civilians were killed in bombings such as Enniskillen, La Mon and in Birmingham, England.

There *was* an investigation into Sammy Devenney's death by Sir Arthur Young, London Metropolitan Police Chief Constable. The official report in 1969, like so many in the years to come (Stalker on shoot-to-kill, Lord Stephens on collusion), was not published. But Young spoke of 'a conspiracy of silence' among senior police officers to conceal the identity of eight members of the RUC who entered Mr Devenney's home on 19 April. Ever since, there has been an official conspiracy of silence about the *actual* cause of the violence.

The prevailing narrative, where blame is apportioned in descending order of responsibility, has the IRA at the top of the list. Yes, the IRA was the British Government's principal protagonist and, once the conflict began, the conflict took on a momentum of its own that no one could have envisaged and went off in many directions. One act could contribute to the triggering of the next violent act. The British paratroopers on Bloody Sunday led to young people joining the IRA, as did the SAS killings at Loughgall. The IRA bombings on Bloody Friday, which caused civilian deaths, led to David Ervine joining the unionist paramilitary Ulster Volunteer Force. British Prime Minister Margaret Thatcher's intransigent attitude to the 1980/1981 H-Blocks' hunger strikes and the deaths of ten republican prisoners fuelled the republican cause.[24]

Successive British Governments, to circumvent what it considered the limits of its own repressive laws, sanctioned British Intelligence to arm unionist paramilitary organisations and run countless agents within loyalist groups in a campaign that was overwhelmingly sectarian in nature. It was aimed at terrorising the nationalist community as reprisal for the IRA campaign. That is why the British Government will not allow meaningful public inquiries: the paper trail leads to 10 Downing Street and Whitehall, headquarters of 'the men of violence'. That is why it hindered the Barron Inquiry into the Dublin and Monaghan bombings by not releasing key documents which, in all likelihood, incriminate British Intelligence.

The statistics of the conflict appear a lot different if one

---

[24] David Ervine was sentenced to eleven years in jail for having explosives. After his release he became a prominent loyalist figure, wasn't afraid to challenge mainstream unionist parties, supported the peace process and became leader of the Progressive Unionist Party. He died from a heart attack in 2007, his loss depriving loyalists of one of their most articulate spokespersons.

looks at the aggregate killed by the British Army, the RUC and loyalist paramilitaries under the rubric of killings in defence of 'the Union'.

Repression is always framed as an understandable reaction to resistance. The reverse is never put—that resistance was a response to repression.

The hierarchy-of-violence narrative, that the outbreak of conflict was principally the IRA's fault, suited successive Irish Governments from Jack Lynch on. In this version, the British were a little bit to blame but Dublin was sympathetic to Britain's predicament and would help it as far as it could, using security co-operation, repression and censorship. Section 31 of the Broadcasting Act prevented people in the Republic from learning the truth and understanding what was really going on. And the unionist parties? They were 'misunderstood' and had poor 'public relations', but Dublin could assure them that it was sympathetic and would respond to their sensitivities. The South's deferral to unionism is not largely out of fondness, respect or concern. It is largely one of opportunism, postponing an overall settlement (for a New Ireland, however it is configured) in order to perpetuate the only state they have known, are familiar and comfortable with, that they control. That is why Fianna Fáil and Fine Gael confront Sinn Féin instead of the DUP and strive to placate unionism.

The cumulative effects of partition, discrimination, humiliation, alienation and repression over successive decades explain the incredible explosion after 1970.

Whatever welcome the British Army initially enjoyed was finally lost in July 1970 by their terrorisation of the oldest and poorest nationalist area in Belfast, the Falls. They surrounded the very people whose streets had been attacked and whose neighbours' homes had been turned to piles of ashes just eleven months earlier. They were searching for guns that republicans had smuggled into west Belfast to prevent another August 1969 unionist pogrom. These weapons had never been fired nor used against the British Army—until these raids. The soldiers first gassed the area from helicopters before the invasion, during which they killed five people, including our youth club manager, Billy Burns, and wounded sixty others. During the Falls Curfew they searched and ransacked five thousand homes, some of which they looted. In others, they desecrated religious emblems and smashed statues. They arrested over two hundred and forty people, some as young as fourteen.

While people cowered in their homes, under orders that they would be shot if they came out, they were further humiliated when two Ulster Unionist ministers, William Long and John Brooke (son of Lord 'I wouldn't have a Catholic about the place' Brookeborough), drove triumphantly through the area, standing up in the back of two British Army vehicles to inspect the operation.

That weekend, the British Army unwittingly recruited several hundred people to the IRA.

The pace of growth of the IRA across the North, in working-class areas and in poor rural communities, didn't all happen at once but came out of direct local experience with the British Army and the Ulster Defence Regiment, and the RUC, or out of solidarity with what was going on in other areas.

Those young people who joined the IRA in the North post-1969 to defend their areas had become increasingly open to the *republican* argument that the British Army was here to defend Stormont and the Northern state; and that the only way you would get your civil rights was by getting national rights too. The fifty-year-old, one-party Unionist Government—the Orange State—was principally underwritten by British law, British finance, British propaganda and British guns.

After the republican split in December 1969, a *provisional* IRA Army Council had been set up to reorganise the Republican Movement. Among the five reasons cited for the split the first was the proposal to recognise Westminster, Stormont and Leinster House. In my opinion, many nationalists and young people felt that the fourth reason should have been the first—'Failure to give maximum possible defence in Belfast and other Northern areas in August 1969.' The men who showed up with guns at the barricades were more important than any orator or polemicist. Republicans from the South also came North—it was an IRA man from Dublin whom I met in a house in the Clonard area who asked me to help set up Radio Free Belfast. During the internment week riots in 1971, I also came across young people from the South who had come to offer whatever help they could. In jail, I was to meet people from Donegal, Cork and Dublin whom I admired for their solidarity because despite having had no direct experience of repression they came north to support the nationalist community.

Those young people who joined the IRA post-1969 did not join because they had strong views on the issue of abstentionism. Nor were they persuaded of the morality of armed struggle by the doctrinal notion that the Army

Council of the IRA was, through tenuous lineage, the *legitimate* government of Ireland. Older republicans—who viewed the 1970s as a continuum of traditional republican struggle—emphasised that the leadership was in direct succession to the Provisional Government of 1916, through the First Dáil of 1919, through the delegation of executive powers in 1938 by seven surviving republican delegates of the Second Dáil of 1921, and so on and so forth. This claim, however cherished, played little or no part in the reasoning or persuasion of recruits. Besides, it was clear (to me anyway) that the vast majority of people in the Twenty-Six Counties, from participation in elections and the separate development of the South, considered the institutions of their state as legitimate and a functioning democracy. Whereas the nationalist community in the North in the degree of its alienation and mistreatment did not identify with the institutions there.

Young people joined the IRA because of what was happening on the street. They didn't join because of Robert Emmet, Pádraig Pearse or Dan Breen but probably because a relative or friend had been burned out of their home, or they'd been abused by a British soldier or an RUC policeman, or had their house wrecked. They understood that the conditions under which they existed were directly related to the nature of the state, and that the nature of the unionist state was directly linked to the partition of Ireland by the British (and decisions that Irish republicans made back then, good or bad).

No one took up arms easily or without qualm. Just as in the War of Independence the Catholic Church condemned resistance, this time they also condemned rioters and even some of the street protests. If alienation from the Catholic Church down South was over 'moral' issues (access to contraception, divorce, the treatment of women), in the North it encompassed church opposition to resistance. Young people felt justified because even the peaceful attempts to resolve the inequalities had been met with state violence and the state admitted no wrong. No map existed of a way out. Young people on the Falls Road had had enough of being treated as second-class, and of now being shot down by British soldiers. They knew what their parents and grandparents had experienced. They were fighting on behalf of oppressed people and it was from such communities that they drew support. This was real and tangible and it was the communities in places like the Bogside or Ballymurphy, Crossmaglen, Bellaghy, Coalisland from which they emerged and upon whom they relied.

The IRA was *not* fighting in the name of the people of the South but, of course, it was *part* of the same struggle for independence and for a complete end to British rule in Ireland, one which had been thwarted by partition.

It was a struggle that would be fought tenaciously and ferociously—unjustifiably, ruthlessly and unconscionably in the eyes of its victims, political opponents and critics. It would be fought for far longer than the Tan War, not least because condensed within the crucible of this small space of the Six Counties were the palpable and ultimate realities of the failure of the British partition of Ireland. Partition had made nationalists worse off than they were before 1920, cut adrift, isolated, forgotten, mistreated, ignored when they were silent, demonised and repressed when they protested. All of the nationalist areas attacked and torched in 1969 had been attacked at the time of partition when hundreds were killed and thousands driven from their homes. The young people's attitude was 'Never again.'

It would be fought until real change had been secured and these underlying issues of the conflict addressed.

The closest we have ever got to an admission that unionism mistreated the nationalist community was former Ulster Unionist Party leader David Trimble in his Nobel Peace Prize acceptance speech in 1998. Referring to the past, he said: 'Ulster Unionists, fearful of being isolated on the island, built a solid house, but it was a cold house for Catholics. And Northern nationalists, although they had a roof over their heads, seemed to us as if they meant to burn the house down. None of us are entirely innocent.'

The 1916 Rising was justified by the conditions throughout Ireland, which *included* the treatment of northern nationalists as attempts were made by the IPP to peacefully secure, through democratic means, Home Rule. The establishing of the Ulster Volunteer Force in the North was what inspired the formation of the Irish Volunteers. If the Rising was about the denial of freedom and British misrule in Ireland, the recent armed struggle in the North was about the denial of the same freedom and a more egregious form of British misrule in the form of partition, with one section of the community permanently privileged over another.

In Ireland's major cities prior to 1916 there was, of course, extreme poverty and high unemployment. There had been two deaths in baton charges during the Dublin Lockout of trade unionists in 1913, which preceded and helped define the radical nature of the Proclamation. There had been three deaths at the hands of the British Army after the Irish Volunteers' Howth gun-running incident in July 1914.

And there had been violence against northern nationalists.

'The unionist majority in Belfast,' writes Dr Brian Feeney in his book *Antrim, The Irish Revolution, 1912-23*, 'looked on the city's Catholic population as the enemy within, scapegoats, hostages for the actions of the home rule leaders in Dublin and Westminster. If the precedents of the lethal civil disturbances in 1886 and 1893 in response to earlier home rule bills were anything to go by, there would be death and destruction in Belfast as a third home rule bill made its way through parliament.'[25]

After disturbances in June 1912, Catholics were driven from their workplaces in Belfast and there were attacks on Catholics in Lisburn, Carrickfergus and Ballyclare.

So, while conditions were to ultimately change for the people of the Twenty-Six Counties, conditions worsened for their co-patriots: fifty years of humiliation; the physical persecution of any outward expression of their identity; discrimination in housing, employment and investment; its minority position entrenched; a people denied access to government or power to change government; deaths at the hands of the RUC, B-Specials, unionist mobs and the

---

[25] Published 2021 by Four Courts Press.

British Army long before the IRA reorganised and launched its armed struggle.

Fianna Fáil and Fine Gael lack the courage to participate in an honest debate about the causes of violence because the truth would trigger other imperatives–dealing with the reality of British Government involvement in bombings and assassinations and probable infiltration of the Republic's institutions and security forces. You can be sure that the British Government—although it had more than enough willing allies in the Southern establishment—recruited agents to influence events and help form public opinion and public perceptions. You would be as naïve as John Redmond to think otherwise.

Such discomfiting truths, if admitted, would leave large numbers of Irish people (particularly those in the South subject to mainstream propaganda and before that Section 31 state censorship) more open to understanding and sympathising with nationalists on the issue of the North.

Evidence of British interference in the Republic of Ireland emerged in 1972 and 1973. Petrol bomb attacks on Garda barracks, a big bank robbery and two car bombs in Dublin (which killed two CIÉ workers) were acts by British agents provocateurs, blamed on the IRA, and aimed at influencing the passage of anti-republican legislation in Leinster

House—the Offences against the State (Amendment) Act—which was the British Government's objective.

In mid-December an Englishman, Alexander Forsey, who had been arrested and charged with possession of ammunition and explosive fuses, gave Gardaí the name of John Wyman, an MI6 agent who regularly visited Dublin. He also said that two of Wyman's agents were Kenneth and Keith Littlejohn (whose extradition from England was being sought for the bank robbery mentioned above). Wyman was arrested, followed by Patrick Crinnion, private secretary to the head of the Special Branch, John Fleming. Crinnion had been passing on Gardaí intelligence on republicans to the British. Instead of furiously reacting to this breach of sovereignty the Irish Ambassador to Britain met with the Prime Minister's private secretary and told him that the Wyman affair presented the Irish Government with a 'public relations' problem. 'O'Sullivan intimated that while it was a matter for the courts, his government would attempt to treat Wyman leniently'.[26]

Court proceedings were held *in camera* and the Minister for Justice Desmond O'Malley withheld evidence that would have led to more serious charges. Wyman and Crinnion were given a cursory three months' sentence, were

---

[26] *The 1972-73 Dublin Bombings* by Margaret Urwin and Niall Meehan, HISTORY IRELAND/ May–June 2018

released and vanished. Forsey was given a suspended sentence and disappeared.

At their extradition hearing the Littlejohns called British Government officials as witnesses to prove they were agents, resulting in the proceedings being heard *in camera*. When extradited Kenneth Littlejohn said that Wyman was his handler and that the violence was aimed at facilitating the passage of the repressive legislation. In a memo to London the British Ambassador had written, 'Two bombs on 1 December clinched the matter.'

The Littlejohns were crooks and gangsters and so their stories were more easily dismissed. They were eventually sentenced for the bank robbery and after serving eight years were released on 'humanitarian grounds'.

Bellaghy, 1997, © Gilles Peress / Magnum

PEACE

Dublin Governments (until the premiership of Albert Reynolds and, in 1998, with major contributions from Bertie Ahern) did a major disservice to peace and were chief among those discouraging Britain from engaging with republicans. This prolonged the conflict in the vain hope that the IRA would be defeated. Republicans always wanted dialogue—which is why from 1971 the IRA called so many ceasefires: Christmas ceasefires, Easter ceasefires, weekend ceasefires and extended ceasefires. These were opportunities that successive, foolhardy British Governments squandered in pursuit of the elusive 'military victory'. In any putative resolution of the conflict, republicans had to be convinced that Britain was 'going down the political road', so to speak, otherwise we were engaging in false hope and were in danger of bequeathing a worse and possibly more bloody legacy to the next generation.

In the early 1990s I was of the view that despite the IRA being better armed than ever and able to fight on indefinitely it would be doing so without necessarily improving the overall prospects for lasting peace but with much further loss of life. Recognising the stalemate would mean entering a ceasefire, fraught as it would be. Generally, there would be a huge sense of relief. But you would need to be patient and steady your nerve in anticipation of opponents provocatively crowing about having seen off another IRA campaign and opponents of peace within the British establishment and intelligence community adroitly attempting to exploit the situation and achieving what they were unable to do through 'Operation Banner', as the British Army military campaign against the IRA was called.

There would be political talks and that would require compromise. After August 1994 I was in despair at the way British Prime Minister John Major and the new Fine Gael Taoiseach, John Bruton, were mishandling this opportunity—Major saying that Sinn Féin had to go through a period of decontamination before it could enter talks. It seemed calculated and aimed at undermining the judgement of Gerry Adams and Martin McGuinness, the main drivers of the ceasefire, and creating an internal crisis and a potentially dangerous split that could divide and diminish the Republican Movement, resulting in feuding and fatalities. While the vast majority of activists and former prisoners supported the peace process, a small number did not. Those who broke away were responsible for the Omagh bombing in August 1998 which killed twenty-nine people.

When this extended edition of *The Good Old IRA* was published in early 2022 the historian Brian Hanley reviewed the book and asked: What's to stop dissident republicans publishing their own *Good Old (Provisional) IRA* to justify a campaign?

There are many reasons: circumstances and conditions have fundamentally changed. The nationalist community no longer feels vanquished, it feels empowered. It is probably more confident now than in any time in the past one hundred years. This is why dissident republicans can get little or no traction: we *have* overcome, and we believe there is a possible peaceful road to a New Ireland. This is why dissidents will never be able to replicate the tempo or magnitude of the IRA campaign. Their armed actions are actually ineffectual by any objective standards and, presumably their own, if they are honest. Any valid political criticisms they have get lost. They are never going to reach negotiating status and they have made it virtually impossible, when they ceasefire (as they will, inevitably), to realise the early release of their prisoners, which is what the republican leadership sought and achieved after the Belfast Agreement.

As is well known, unity is strength. There is strength in numbers and it has been the loyalty of the republican base, and the loyalty of the bulk of former republican activists and ex-prisoners, which has seen republicans through this chapter in struggle.

The state we live in, in the North, is not the state we were born into and grew up in. It has, as I said, radically changed—but, of course, it has not changed radically enough. We still have major problems socially, economically and politically, but none that we cannot redress through skill, good political leadership and patience. They cannot be resolved simply through the confines of the Six-County state. The political arrangements that underpin the ceasefire give nationalists a role in government as of right. That is necessary because there are too many indications that unionist parties have not shaken off their sectarian heritage, especially when you consider the regular public insults towards nationalists (see *A Culture of Sectarian Discrimination*, pages 102-108). Though they might reverse their position, the inability of the leaders of the DUP and UUP before the Assembly elections in May 2022 to state that they would accept the democratic outcome and respect Sinn Féin leader Michelle O'Neill as First Minister is a case in point.

The huge task we face is to un-partition this island, is to overturn not just a state embedded within British constitutional law and supported by violence for almost a hundred years, but to compel the political leaderships in the Republic of Ireland to face its responsibilities towards *all* of the Irish people.

Irish republicanism rattles their complacency and historic disregard of the North. The rise in support for Sinn Féin's progressive and radical policies threatens to upend the dominance that those parties have enjoyed since their acceptance of partition. Their 'pride' in the Republic of Ireland (their *Ireland*) has stunted their vision about what is our due in relation to justice, political and economic freedom and what can be achieved.

British and unionist attitudes to republicanism are understandable, both from an ideological point of view and given what the IRA campaign inflicted on life and property. We are still undoing the damage which partition wrought on our people, Catholic and Protestant and of every other persuasion, who from their respective positions paid heavily for this division and the political mistakes of the past. We have all hurt each other but we have, undeniably, come a long way. Peace has come 'dropping slow'.

Anyone who has read the book *Curious Journey* by Tim O'Grady and Kenneth Griffith, an oral history of the Tan War period, in which IRA veterans express their regret (and sometimes weep) for the suffering and death their actions caused—whilst not eschewing the stance they took—will realise that those men and women were the first to acknowledge the ambiguities and complexities all conflicts throw up.

The past has not gone away and history remains hotly contested.

This book is a necessary riposte to those political parties in the Republic of Ireland who, in their current competition with Sinn Féin, continue to rely on the fallacy of 'Our violence was good, yours bad.' They choose to ignore the reality that conflict in Ireland is a direct result of British interference in our sovereignty, but as political cowards they recoil from apportioning blame to Britain.

A complaint made by some republicans when *The Good Old IRA* first appeared was that although IRA actions were listed there was little or no mention of repression, of the British executions, killings, arrests, torture of prisoners, curfews, sacking of towns, or reprisals against individuals or property. Referencing those would make explicable the magnitude and nature of the conflict and cast IRA actions in an understandable light.

The IRA operations listed are recorded in this way, without context, quite often reflecting a British propaganda slant, precisely because that was how the IRA campaign in the North was also largely reported in the mainstream media.

What follows is a representative sample of IRA operations during the Tan War, also known as the War of Independence. One can make up one's own mind on the morality of Irish men and women taking up the gun in the circumstances of that period, just as one can query the morality of what the IRA did from 1970 until its final ceasefire. What is undeniable is that the Tan War operations have multiple parallels with the IRA's campaign in the North—quite simply because it was the continuation of the same struggle.

Prisoners released from Frongoch Prison Camp arrive in
Dublin to a tumultuous reception, 1917

The Good Old IRA

1917/18

After their release from Frongoch internment camp in Wales in December 1916, the Volunteers returned to Ireland where their comrades had begun reorganising the Movement and preparing for the next phase of struggle.

In March, 1917, Irish Republican Brotherhood member John Joe 'Tosser' Neylon opened fire and wounded RIC Constable Johns.

In June 1917, the remaining prisoners were released as part of a general amnesty.

Just months after his release, Thomas Ashe, IRB, was arrested and charged with making a speech in County Longford in contravention of the Defence of the Realm Act. He was sentenced to two years' hard labour. He went on hunger strike, demanding political status, and on 25 September, as he was being forcibly fed for the fifth time, food entered his lungs, causing asphyxiation and death. His body lay in state at the City Hall, dressed in his Volunteer republican uniform. Thirty-thousand mourners filed past his open coffin to pay their respects.

In his short oration, Michael Collins implicitly stated that the way forward was to be through armed struggle: 'That volley which we have just heard is the only speech which is proper to make above the grave of a dead Fenian.'

Collins authorised the resumption of gun-running, the purchase of munitions and the acquisition of gelignite.

Reflecting on the early revolutionary period and the decision to wage guerrilla warfare, Ernie O'Malley wrote in his memoir, *The Singing Flame*: 'I was called to order by Cathal Brugha for stating that we had never consulted the feelings of the people. If so, we would never have fired a shot. If we gave them a good strong lead, they would follow.'

In the various by-elections from 1917 on (won by Sinn Féin), the most bitter and often violent opposition to the republicans came from the Redmondite Irish Parliamentary Party which contained many former British Army soldiers. Sinn Féin election workers were physically attacked, six being badly beaten outside the Old Grand Hotel in Ennis, County Clare, by Redmondites and members of the Ancient Order of Hibernians.

Volunteers throughout Ireland defied British authority through secretly drilling. In Clare, Volunteers began openly parading men in uniform in the presence of the Royal Irish Constabulary. This resulted in large-scale arrests.

In March 1918, the Volunteers established a General Headquarters Staff. The Volunteers' newspaper, *An tÓglach*, reported 'the unanimous decision of the Executive of the Irish Volunteers to resist conscription to the death with all the military force and warlike resources at our command'.

In the December general election, Sinn Féin scored a landslide victory and commits to establishing Dáil Éireann.

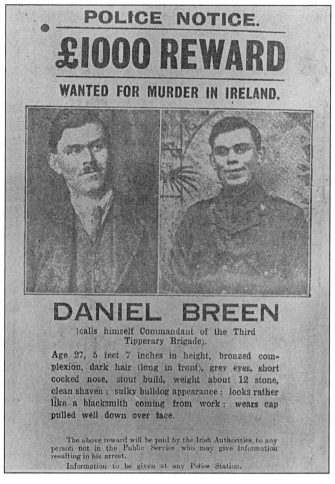

POLICE NOTICE.

£1000 REWARD

WANTED FOR MURDER IN IRELAND.

DANIEL BREEN

(calls himself Commandant of the Third
Tipperary Brigade).

Age 27, 5 feet 7 inches in height, bronzed complexion, dark hair (long in front), grey eyes, short cocked nose, stout build, weight about 12 stone, clean shaven; sulky bulldog appearance; looks rather like a blacksmith coming from work; wears cap pulled well down over face.

The above reward will be paid by the Irish Authorities, to any person not in the Public Service who may give information resulting in his arrest.

Information to be given at any Police Station.

1919

Soloheadbeg

Two RIC police officers were shot dead on 21 January while transporting gelignite at Soloheadbeg, County Tipperary. One of them, Constable J. McDonnell (50), was a widower with four children. He was a native of County Mayo.

Arms raid

Alfred Parsons (60) was shot dead during an arms raid on his shop at 146 Richmond Road, Dublin, on 11 March. He was shot with a revolver and staggered out onto the street before dying.

Dáil Directive

In April 1919, a Dáil directive commanded IRA units throughout the country to begin the boycott, intimidation and harassment of police officers and their families, as the RIC was seen as the eyes and ears of the British Government.

Limerick Workhouse

An RIC policeman, Martin O'Brien (50), was shot dead on 6 April at Limerick Workhouse during the rescue of Robert Byrne, who was on hunger strike. Constable O'Brien was married with one child.

Not 'a moment's notice'

Seán Hogan was rescued from the Thurles to Cork train at Knocklong, County Limerick, on 13 May. Sergeant Peter Wallace, of Curraghroe, County Roscommon, and Constable Michael Enright were both shot dead during the rescue. Constable Jeremiah Ring swore at the inquest that the men who rushed the train shouted, 'Hands up!' and then fired immediately. 'We didn't get a moment's notice what to do.'

'The shooting of the policemen was a crime against God and a crime against Ireland,' said the Reverend Dr Harty.

Shot in the back

RIC District Inspector Hunt (50) was shot dead in the square at Thurles on 23 June by armed men. He was on duty at Thurles Races. He was shot twice in the back. A twelve-year-old boy was wounded in the knee.

'After the shooting a large crowd gathered but did not help. They jeered and laughed.'

— *Irish News*

'Foul crime'

Sergeant Philip Brady (48) was shot dead at Lorrha, County Tipperary, on 2 September. He was married with six children. He was shot while on patrol with two other policemen. Shots rang out without warning and Brady fell dead. At his funeral the parish priest denounced in the strongest terms the people who sent Sergeant Brady to meet his maker: 'Every right-thinking man in the church and state must condemn this foul crime.'

Sunday ambush

In Fermoy, County Cork, on Sunday, 7 September, a group of seventeen soldiers of the King's Shropshire Light Infantry were walking to church when they were attacked by a group of twelve or thirteen men. Revolver shots rang out and Private William Jones, a native of Carmarthen, Wales, fell dead. Three other soldiers were wounded. The soldiers were carrying rifles but had no ammunition for them. The attackers made off with thirteen rifles.

The inquest found that no murder had taken place because the attackers didn't come with the intention to kill but to steal rifles. The Most Reverend Dr Brown, Bishop of Cloyne, said: 'The little band of soldiers had given no cause of provocation; they were proceeding in orderly and inoffensive manner to their religious Sunday service.'

The Catholic Church

Courtesy An Phoblacht/Republican News

'It is often said that the Catholic Church will never support a revolution until it is successful'
— Oliver P. Rafferty, S.J.

1867 Bishop Moriarty of Kerry denounced the Fenians as criminals saying: 'When we look down into the fathomless depth of this infamy of the heads of the Fenian conspiracy, we must acknowledge that eternity is not long enough, nor hell hot enough to punish such miscreants.'

1886 Archbishop Thomas Croke of Cashel contributed five pounds towards the cost of a monument erected in the grounds of Limerick Cathedral to the 1867 Fenians, the 'Manchester Martyrs'.

1916 Seven bishops publicly condemned the 1916 Rising. The *Irish Catholic* at the time described the Rising as both insane and criminal. 'Pearse was a man of ill-balanced mind, if not actually insane... selecting him as "chief magistrate" was enough to create doubts about the sanity of those who approved... no reason to lament that its perpetrators have met the fate universally reserved for traitors.'

1966 A Solemn High Mass was held in Dublin's Pro-Cathedral to mark the anniversary of Pearse the Insane, and the 1916 Rising. Afterwards, the Garden of Remembrance (a permanent memorial to the Easter 1916 patriots) is officially opened by de Valera and is blessed by Archbishop of Dublin, Dr John Charles McQuaid.

1919 Monsignor Ryan, the Parish Priest of Tipperary, denounced the Soloheadbeg ambush as a criminal act perpetrated by a gang of murders. He said, 'God help poor Ireland if she follows this deed of blood. But let us give her the lead in our indignant denunciation of this crime against our Catholic civilization.'

2021 A Mass of Remembrance was celebrated by the Archbishop of Cashel and Emly, Kieran O'Reilly, at Solohead Church. Culture Minister Josepha Madigan laid a wreath in remembrance of all who suffered and died during the struggle for independence. She said: 'I commend the efforts and commitment of the Solohead Parish Centenary Commemoration Committee and the Third Tipperary Brigade Old IRA Commemoration Committee who have ensured that today's ceremony is authentic, appropriate, inclusive and meaningful.'

1919–21 Bishop of Cork, Daniel Coholan, excommunicated the IRA.

The Catholic hierarchy came out in favour of the 1921 Treaty— before even Dáil Éireann had voted on the issue—joining with the Southern business classes who were never happy at the progressive nature of the economic and social principles espoused in the First Dáil's Democratic Programme.

1923 Bishop Joseph MacRory denounced and encouraged the excommunication of anti-Treaty republicans for attacking a democratically-elected government during the Civil War in Ireland.

1936 Cardinal (former Bishop) Joseph MacRory supported and blessed those attacking a democratically-elected government during the Civil War in Spain.

1918 Terence MacSwiney, while on hunger strike receives Holy Communion daily. Upon his death he is granted a full Catholic funeral and burial.

1922 Terence MacSwiney's sister, Mary, while on hunger strike is refused Holy Communion. Catholic Archbishop of Dublin

Edward Byrne told the prisoner she was breaking a divine law by hunger striking: 'All who participate in such crimes are guilty of the gravest sins and may not be absolved nor admitted to Holy Communion.'

1969-94 Bishop (later Cardinal) Cahal B. Daly in his 1973 book, *Violence in Ireland and Christian Conscience*, writes, 'A Christian is not obliged to hold that recourse to violence is in all circumstances and of necessity wrong.' The reason for this initially surprising preface soon becomes clear as he segues into the Good Old IRA Vs the Wicked Modern IRA narrative.

'I am personally convinced that our fight for national freedom was just and necessary. The heroism both of soldiers and civilians in that struggle wrote a glorious chapter in our history.'

'It will be retorted that modern Irish democracy grew precisely out of the barrels of the rifles of 1916. But let us never forget that the revolutionary violence was endorsed and the subsequent struggle legitimated by the most democratic and most conclusive election perhaps ever held in Ireland. The Army that fought for freedom was the Army of the elected Parliament and government of the Irish people.'

'When someone condemns violence in Ireland now it is often charged that he must consequently condemn the violence used by the patriots of 1916. The charge is unfounded. I am not condemning the rising of 1916. I am simply saying that this is not 1916. This is 1972.'

'We were obliged to resort to violence in order to secure our just freedom... we were morally right to resort to violence for that just cause.'

In the 1980s Cahal Daly regularly spoke to British Government ministers (who had no mandate) whilst refusing to meet Gerry Adams, even after he was elected MP for West Belfast. By discouraging dialogue Daly's stance arguably prolonged the conflict. The late Ulster Unionist MP Harold McCusker caustically described Daly as 'the vicar-general of the SDLP.'

Bayonets and bullets

'If they [the British] are going to rule this country by the bayonet and the bullet, they will get the bayonet and the bullet in return.'

— Arthur Griffith, *Irish News*, 6 September

Innocent horse

'A horse at Rearcross was found shot dead in the stable. It is stated that the animal was used to draw fuel to the local police.'

— *Irish News*, 23 September

'An official list of outrages'

'The Press Association states: There was issued from Dublin Castle on Saturday night a tabulated return of the outrages in Ireland attributed to the Sinn Féin movement from May 1st 1916 to September 30th last. This gives a total of 1,293 outrages as follows: - Murder 16 (14 military or police officials and two civilians); firing at the person 66; assaults 60; raids for arms etc 478; incendiary fires 55; injury to property 261; firing into dwellings 30; threatening letters 141; miscellaneous offences 186.

'In Munster alone the outrages totalled 624, including 11 murders. Leinster's record is 377 outrages.'

— *Irish News*, 13 October

Cliffoney Ambush

Amongst four RIC policemen killed in an ambush on 25 October was fifty-one-year old Sergeant Patrick Perry, from Boyle, Roscommon, a married man whose wife was expecting their eleventh child.

Warning

The following are some extracts from a poster distributed in the Macroom district of County Cork in October 1919:

'The people in this area are warned that, for their own safety and in the interests of their country, they should avoid absolutely all communications of a friendly nature with members of the RIC. This force of men is specially organised for the maintenance in our downtrodden country of a tyrannical foreign government by a system of spying and corruption unrivalled in any land.

'The police who come from amongst the people themselves are traitors to their own flesh and blood, sworn to spare neither parent, brother, sister, nor wife in the discharge of their degrading duty—the overthrow of the God-given right of their fellow countrymen. They should therefore be avoided as more dangerous than the plague and more ruinous than any other group of ruffians to the morals of society.

'Let no Irish man or woman with a sense of principle or honour be seen speaking to, saluting, or in any way tolerating the existence of a peeler either in public or in private. ''Beware! This is not an appeal but an order from the Irish Republican Government. To those who ignore it will be meted the punishment of traitors.'

Barrack knock

At Ballivor, County Meath, Constable William Agar was shot dead on 31 October when he answered a knock at the door of the barracks to armed and masked men who then cleared the barracks of arms and ammunition. Constable Agar was married only five months. An old man who was going to collect water from a pump near the barracks saw a number of armed men. When they saw him, one of them shouted, 'Go back! If you come on you will be shot!'

Old man beaten

Lieutenant Colonel F. St Tottenham's home near Cork city was raided for arms in November. About six armed and masked men entered the house, with others outside. When the old man refused to give up his gun he was thrown around and beaten. He was given two black eyes and was finally knocked down. The men eventually made off with the guns. The colonel was seventy years old.

Attempt to kill Lord French

In a failed ambush on the three-car convoy of Lord French, Lord Lieutenant of Ireland, on 19 December, IRA Volunteer Martin Savage was killed in return fire. Dublin Pro-Cathedral refused to allow Savage's body to rest there. St Laurence's, his parish church in Grangegorman, also refused to take his remains. He was eventually buried in his home town of Ballisodare, Sligo, in a funeral attended by thousands of people. Holy Ireland 'shall never be regenerated by deeds of blood or raised up by the hand of the midnight assassination … [the perpetrators] can lay no claim to the name of a patriot', said Cardinal Logue.

Free press

At 10am on 21 December, about thirty or forty men, some armed, entered the *Irish Independent* premises and wrecked the printing presses. A note condemning the *Irish Independent* story on the Lord French attack was handed to a member of the staff during the raid.

'The outrage is attributed to adverse comment on the Sinn Féin movement.'

— *Irish News*

IRA grenade factory in Cavan.

1920

Visitors

'During a raid for arms on the home of a farmer at Ballagh, Enniscorthy, County Wexford, on the night of Saturday, 14 February, the farmer's wife, Mrs Ellen Morris, was shot in the chest from point-blank range and died almost instantly. Mrs Morris was shot when she tried to push the leader of the raiders out of the cottage, telling them to clear out with their pop guns, not to be annoying people, and that there were no guns in the house. The leader of the raiders raised his gun and shot her in the chest.

'When one of the occupants of the house tried to go for a priest he was told by the leader of the raiders, "You will go for no priest: she does not want one, and if you or anyone else leaves this house within two hours the same end awaits you." The raiders then left. It was an hour before anyone left the house.'

— *Irish News*, 16 February

Ex-soldier

Harry Timothy Quinlisk was found shot dead at Ballyphehane, County Cork, on 20 February. He had been shot nine times. Quinlisk was an ex-soldier and a native of County Waterford.

The Pope and Sinn Féin

'The daily paper, *Don Finchotte*, understands that the Vatican is about to make representations to the Irish Episcopate and the Apostolic delegation in Washington, insisting that clergymen on both sides of the Atlantic with Sinn Féin sympathies should leave the revolutionary movement and work for pacification or at least a return to legality.'

— *Reuters*, Paris, 25 February

Spy

John Charles Byrne (34), married with four or five children, was found shot dead in Hampstead Lane, leading from Ballymun Road, Glasnevin, to the Model Farm, Glasnevin, Dublin. He had been shot seven times.

'At first it was thought that Byrne, an Englishman living in Essex, was shot while on holidays in Ireland, but later reports suggested that he was a spy.'

— *Irish News*, 3 March

Shopping

Constable Heanue (22) was shot and seriously wounded at Ragg village near Thurles, County Tipperary, on 4 March. He died on 5 March in Tipperary Military Hospital. Heanue was in a shop buying groceries when he was shot from behind without warning.

Visitor killed

Martin Cullinane was shot dead while visiting John Lardiner's house at Ardsheamoe, Corofin, County Clare, on 4 March. It happened during a raid for guns by armed and masked men. When the raiders arrived, the occupants of the house were too frightened to let them in. When they eventually gained admission they started to search the house and no resistance was offered. Cullinane was by the fireplace when a shot came through the front door and hit him in the chest. The shot had come from one of the raiders who was covering the outside of the house. When the raiders upstairs heard the shot they ran down and, seeing the dying man, ran out of the house and away. Cullinane (45) was married and had four young children; the youngest was two years old.

Unarmed

Constable James Rock and Constable Healy were shot dead in an attack on Tuesday, 16 March, at Toomevara, County Tipperary. The incident took place in the square of the village which was crowded with people returning from novena devotions at the time. Rock and Healy were also just coming from the novena devotions. They were unarmed at the time and were shot from behind without warning. After the first shots, Rock lay wounded on the ground and Healy ran to the safety of the police barracks. The gunmen fired after Healy and then turned their attention again to Rock, who was lying wounded in the middle of the road. He begged for mercy but the gunmen fired three more shots at him and killed him. Healy died later.

Parliamentary reply

'Victims since January 1919. List of murders, attempted murders and barracks attacked:

'In addition, there have been 25 attacks on police barracks.

'Since figures were compiled, two more RIC men have been killed.'

	Murders	Attempted murders
RIC	16	65
DMP	6	17
Soldiers	2	4
Other govt servants	1	3
TOTAL	25	89

Stored RIC bicycles

Cornelius Kelly, a tailor, was shot dead at Caherdaniel, County Kerry, on Wednesday night, 17 March, by a party of masked men. The local police barracks was closed last week and the police had left their bicycles in Kelly's house.

Pope's Quay

Constable Joseph Murtagh (40) was shot dead at Pope's Quay, Cork city, on 19 March.

Murtagh, who was off-duty and at home on leave, was walking along the quayside when a number of shots rang out. He was hit by eight, death being instantaneous.

Murtagh had twenty-four years' service, was a widower and left three children. He was a native of County Meath.

Tomás Mac Curtain, Lord Mayor of Cork, was shot dead in his home two hours after this attack.

Off-duty

Private Brian Fergus Molloy, an off-duty soldier, was shot dead at the corner of Wicklow Street and Andrew Street, Dublin, on 24 March.

He was walking along the street when two men came walking up quickly behind him. They shot him in the head and he fell dead on the spot.

Magistrate killed

Resident Magistrate Alan Bell was shot dead on the morning of 26 March after being dragged from a tram car on which he was going to his duties at Dublin Castle. As the tram arrived at the corner of Simmonscourt Square and Merrion Road, one man stopped it and immobilised it. At this point, three men rose from their seats and went towards Bell. One of the men was heard to say, 'Come on, Mr Bell. Your time has come.'

Bell refused to move, so the three men dragged him off the tram. As they stepped off, they were met by three others. Bell was shot three times in the head. He died instantly.

Procession

Sergeant Patrick Fennerty (53), an RIC policeman, was shot and very badly wounded at Balbriggan, County Dublin, on 14 April as a Sinn Féin procession, celebrating the release of hunger strikers from Mountjoy, was passing. He died on 16 April.

Creamery killing

Constable Patrick Foley (25), of Annascaul, County Kerry, was found shot dead in a creamery yard on 16 April. He had been missing since 14 April. He was tied and his eyes were bandaged. He had been shot twenty-six times.

Foley, who was stationed in Galway, was off-duty and at home on leave at the time of the shooting.

Off-duty

Constable Martin Clifford was shot dead near his home at Waterville, County Kerry, on 17 April. He was off-duty and at home on leave at the time.

Mass killing

RIC Sergeant Patrick Carroll was shot dead while leaving church after Mass at Kilmihill, County Clare (West), on 18 April.

Detective

RIC Detective Constable Laurence Dalton (26) was shot dead in Mountjoy Street, Dublin, on 21 April. He had six years' service. Mrs Ivers, an elderly woman, was wounded during the attack.

In the field

DMP Constable Michael McCarthy was shot in Cork on 22 April. He died on 24 April at Cork Military Hospital. McCarthy was off-duty and at home on leave working in a field when two men approached him. They produced guns, shot him and ran off.

Haircut

Seven masked men, one armed with a revolver, entered the Keegan family home in Cloondarone, Galway, after midnight, 30 April. They grabbed Bridget Keegan, who had fainted, and took her out to the yard in her nightdress where they chopped her hair off with a shears. They told her sister Margaret this is

what Bridget got 'for going with Tommies.' Margaret said one
of the men while cutting off Bridget's hair was singing, 'We
are out for Ireland free.' They also threatened to cut off her
ears.

(There was a similar case in Castletownroche, Cork, in June
1920 when approximately sixteen masked men attacked two
young women in their home for 'entertaining military
officers.')

Failed to answer

William J. McCabe (42), a single man, and a gardener to
the Right Honourable Laurence Waldron PC (Peace
Commissioner), was shot dead at Strathmore Road, Killiney,
near his employer's residence on 13 May. It was believed to
be connected to the burning of Ballybrack RIC Barracks
which happened at the same time. It was thought that
McCabe failed to answer a challenge or disregarded a
warning given by scouts of the party that destroyed the
barracks. He was shot twice.

Derry shooting

On the night of 15 May Sergeant Denis Moroney pursued
rioters after disturbances between the loyalist Fountain area
and nationalists from Bridge Street. He was hit by shots
fired from a revolver and died at the Metropole Hotel.

Burned to death

Sergeant T. Kane and Constable J Morton were burned to death during an attack on the RIC Barracks at Kilmallock, County Limerick, on 28 May. The charred remains of the two men were found the next day. Kane was aged about fifty and had thirty years' service. He left a wife and a large family. Morton (48), a native of Thurles, left a wife and two children. He also had thirty years' service.

Riddled

John Dwyer was found shot dead on the roadside at Annesgrove, near Drumbane, County Tipperary, on 14 July. He worked as a caretaker at Annesgrove House which been burned to the ground in the expectation that the military were about to occupy it. He had been associated with an eviction, had received threatening letters and the public had been warned not to associate with him. His body was riddled with bullets. He left a widow and a large family.

Bandon Mass

On Sunday, 25 July, Sergeant William Mulhern (35), married, was shot dead in the porch of the church during Mass

Body in a bog

On 29 July, the badly-decomposed body of RIC Constable Thomas Hannon was found in a bog at Ballyduff, near Tullamore, County Offaly. There was a bullet wound in the right temple, his hands were tied behind his back, and he had a sack over his head. Hannon had been missing for over a year. He had left his barracks on 19 July 1920, unarmed and in civilian clothes. It is believed he was held captive for some time before being shot. He was married with five children.

Westland Row

The Right Honourable Frank Brooke PC, ex-serviceman and advisor to Lord French, was shot dead in a room at Westland Row Railway Station (now Pearse Street Station), Dublin, between 12.15 pm and 12.30 pm on 30 July. Between six and eight men entered the room, singled out Brooke and shot him dead. The one other man in the room, Arthur Cotton, whom Brooke was talking to, narrowly escaped injury. The gunmen left but one returned and fired more shots into the dead man.

Cloomore

A young man, aged about twenty two, was found blindfolded and shot. His hands were tied behind his back.

Around his neck a white pasteboard was tied with twine on it and in black letters was the word 'spy'. His body was discovered by a creamery worker named John Mullane at Cloomore near Drumcollogher, County Limerick, on 1 August. He had been shot six times.

Lisburn killing

District Inspector Oswald Swanzy was shot dead just after 1 pm on Sunday, 22 August, when returning from service in Christ Church Cathedral, Lisburn. The street was crowded at the time and Swanzy was walking with two other people when four men came rushing at him, pushing other people out of the way. They confronted him at the corner of Railway Street, started firing and hit him five times. He died immediately.

Swanzy's father was a native of Castleblayney, County Monaghan, and his mother was from Lisburn. The Most Reverend Dr MacRory, Bishop of Down and Conor, said that it was a particularly indefensible and savage act and as such he deeply deplored and strongly condemned it. He believed that nobody from the diocese of Down and Conor had anything whatsoever to do with it.

Dundalk shooting

In Jocelyn Street, Dundalk, on 22 August, about six or seven men attacked a four-man police patrol. Constable Brennan was killed and two others wounded.

'Am I to be told that this is an act of war? That it is lawful to shoot on sight anyone wearing a policeman's uniform and honestly discharging a policeman's duties? I prefer to call it by its true name: a cool, deliberate, wilful murder, pure and simple.'

— Cardinal Logue.

Donegal JP

Justice of the Peace Major G.H. Johnstone was shot dead in his own home at Eden, about ten miles from Glenties, County Donegal. Johnstone was sitting in his dining room about 10.30 pm when two men, armed and wearing masks, entered the room and shot him dead. Johnstone had lived there all his life and had taken no part in politics. He was seventy years old.

Death by drowning

An ex-soldier called Jim Kenny was executed in Graiguenamanagh, County Kilkenny, on 30 August. He was taken by boat into the middle of the River Barrow and drowned. He had been found guilty of passing information to the British about IRA activities.

Dungarvan

On 30 August, a house was raided for arms about nine miles from Dungarvan, County Waterford, by about twenty men. The occupier's two sons resisted but one of them was shot in the chest and died soon after. The other son was overpowered and the men made off with the guns.

Monaghan

The house of Jack Hazlett was raided at Kilnadrain near Monaghan town on 31 August. The raid was for guns. When Hazlett resisted the raiders he was shot through the neck. There was little hope held out for his survival. Hazlett later died from his wounds.

Aghafin Raid

During a number of raids for arms on the homes of unionist sympathisers in County Monaghan Aghafin House owned by John Madden was entered by men wearing disguises. Upstairs they called upon Madden's sister Isabel to open her locked bedroom door. Miss Madden allegedly fired a shot to scare of the raiders. They returned fire and she was shot in the abdomen and seriously injured. The men left with their prize of a few shotguns and ammunition, and a service rifle.

Wake

On the night of 5 September, two policemen (who were brothers) went home on leave to bury a relative at Colghone, Dingle, County Kerry. They were in a neighbour's house when a party of armed men arrived. The policemen escaped by a back door accompanied by John Moriarty (17), a son of the farmer in whose house they were in. The intruders opened fire on the three escaping men, killing Moriarty.

Drumclogher

Patrick Daly, a farm labourer, was found shot dead in a field near Drumclogher on 17 September with a note bearing the word 'spy' pinned to the body. He had been abducted on 30 July.

'For Kilkee'

Captain Lendrum Resident Magistrate, Kilrush, County Clare, was abducted on 22 September on his way to Ennistymon Petty Sessions after an exchange of shots in which he was mortally wounded. The Tans threatened to burn villages unless he was found. On 1 October Lendrum's body, wrapped in a sheet inside a roughly-made coffin was recovered beside the local railway line. A note pinned to the coffin said, 'For Kilkee' and had the message, 'he died for a foreign Hunnish Government.' According to *The Times*, 'The body and the sheet showed traces of having been in the sea for some days.' It was also rumoured that the wounded magistrate had been buried up to his neck on a beach, waiting for the tide to come in. An autopsy report said that he had drowned. He was a native of Trillick, County Tyrone.

Beehive Attack

Two RIC men were patrolling the Falls Road close to midnight on 25 September when they were challenged by gunmen outside the Beehive Bar and ordered to hand over their weapons. When they refused they were shot by the IRA. One of the RIC men, thirty-five-year old Thomas Leonard, a married man with three children from Roscommon, died undergoing surgery in the Royal Victoria Hospital.

Skibbereen

Samuel Richard Shannon, Lissaclarig, near Skibbereen, County Cork, died in Cork Hospital on 1 October from wounds received three weeks previously. The residence of his father was raided for arms by masked men but the occupants resisted. The raiders disappeared. The next morning, when Mr Shannon and his son were leaving the house, they were fired on by masked men and the son was fatally wounded.

Cork bombs

Between eight and nine o'clock on Friday morning, 8 October, a military lorry was attacked in Barrack Street, Cork. Bombs were thrown at the lorry, killing one soldier and wounding three others. Three men and a woman were also wounded in the attack. The attack happened as the lorry, which was carrying supplies to Elizabeth Fort, was passing the corner of Cove Street. After the four bombs were thrown, the attackers opened fire with revolvers.

Watchmaker

James Mahony, a travelling watchmaker, entered Skibbereen Workhouse on 13 October. On leaving, he was met by an armed and masked man who shot him three times in the head. He died almost immediately. He had been arrested two months previously by Sinn Féin police but escaped and had reported the republicans to the military.

Special duty

R1C Sergeant Roche, stationed in County Tipperary, was shot at the corner of Capel Street and Ormond Quay, Dublin, on 17 October. He had come up to Dublin on special duty to identify the body of Seán Treacy, who had been shot dead in Talbot Street on 14 October.

He was approached by some men who shot and wounded him. He was able to run away but was pursued by the gunmen who eventually shot him in the face, killing him. Ellen Allen (15) and Daniel Reed, an elderly shopkeeper, were both wounded by the gunmen.

Tempo raid

Philip Breen, a civilian, was killed after an attack on Tempo RIC Barracks, County Fermanagh, on 25 October. Several of the raiders were leaving the town when one of them fired a number of shots back up the street. Breen was hit and died shortly afterwards.

Daughter shot

Miss Kathleen Kelly, daughter of Mr R. Kelly, a retired member of the RIC, was shot and wounded in Nenagh, County Tipperary, on 29 October, as she walked down the street with another woman.

Bloody Sunday

Fourteen policemen and 'G-men' were killed in Dublin on Sunday, 21 November—'Bloody Sunday'. Nine of those killed were still in their pyjamas and some were killed in the presence of their wives. The wife of officer Captain Newbury died during labour and a stillbirth three weeks after her husband's violent death.

(In reprisal, at Croke Park during the All-Ireland GAA football final later that day, British forces killed or fatally wounded fourteen civilians and wounded at least sixty others.)

Among the gunmen to enter 119 Lower Baggot Street was Seán Lemass, future Fianna Fáil TD and Taoiseach. Another was Matty MacDonald who described what happened:

'We knocked at the front door a maid came along. "I have a letter from the Castle, will you deliver this note to Captain Bagelly [Baggallay], a one legged man," I said. The maid pointing and in we went. We tapped at the door, opened it and walked in. There were three of us. Bagelly was in bed. Lemass, Jimmy and I. I was kind of scared. "Captain Bagelly?" "That's my name." "I suppose you know what we came for. We came for you." He was the Judge Advocate General. "I suppose you've come for my guns," he said. One of us, Jimmy Brennan hid it under the bed and he reached behind for it... Slugs and a little more was our reply. "Get up." He was in pyjamas. Lemass and Jimmy and I fired two in the head from the three guns. I heard the maid screaming afterwards but I was told she was alright.'

At 117 Morehampton Road a ten-year-old boy at the family boarding house answered a knock on his front door. Eight IRA men rushed passed him and up the stairs. Besides killing an ex-soldier they also shot dead the landlord, Thomas Smith, and severely wounded his brother-in-law John Caldow.

IRA Volunteer Vinny Byrne described the killing of two agents at 38 Upper Mount Street. He knocked on the front door. A servant girl answered and he asked to see Captain Bennett or Lieutenant Ames. She said that they were asleep and went to close the door but he stuck his foot in the door and, claiming he was their friend, was allowed to come in. The servant indicated their bedrooms. 'She was doing very good, you know?' he laughed, when recollecting it years later. And then, having extracted the men from their rooms, 'I put the two of them up against the wall. I said, "The Lord have mercy on your souls," and I plugged the two of them.'

In the Gresham Hotel Captain McCormack was having breakfast in bed and reading *The Irish Field* when the gunmen shot him in the head, neck, wrist and groin. On the next floor gunmen shot dead Leonard Wilde who was posing as a commercial traveller.

Michael Collins justified the killings. He said, 'My one intention was the destruction of the undesirables who continued to make miserable the lives of ordinary decent citizens… If I had a second motive it was no more than a feeling such as I would have for a dangerous reptile. By their destruction the very air is made sweeter. That should be the future's judgement on this particular event. For myself, my conscience is clear. There is no crime in detecting and destroying in war-time, the spy and the informer. I have paid them back in their own coin.'

Devotions

RIC Head Constable J. J. Kearney, Canal Street Barracks, died on 22 November after being shot the day before in Needham Street, Newry, on his way home from evening devotions in the Dominican Church.

Waterfall Railway Station

On 22 November, three British soldiers travelling in plainclothes, two of whom were intelligence officers, were taken off a train, shot and killed and secretly buried by the

IRA in County Cork. Their bodies have never been
recovered.

Discharged soldier
Thomas Downing, an ex-soldier and the son of an ex-RIC
man, was kidnapped while going to a Discharged Soldiers'
and Sailors' meeting on 23 November. He was executed as a
spy. His body has never been found.

Kilmichael ambush
Eighteen Auxiliary policemen were shot dead in an ambush
at Kilmichael, County Cork, on Sunday, 28 November. One
of those who escaped, Cecil Guthrie, was caught the
following day by the IRA. He was beaten to death and his
body buried in a bog. His wife Irene who was eight months
pregnant at the time of his abduction placed a notice in the
Irish Independent in January 1921, in the hope that he was a
prisoner, which read: 'Cecil, Little Dorothy arrived safely.
Irene.' Guthrie's body was recovered in 1926 following a tip-
off.
'They had gone down into the mire to destroy us and our
Nation, and down after them we had to go.'
   - Tom Barry, Cork Brigade IRA

Cork attack

One Auxiliary cadet, S. K. Chapman, 490 London Road, Westcliffe-on-Sea (late of 4th Battalion, London Regiment), was wounded along with eleven others in an ambush on military lorries at Dillon's Cross, Cork city, on 12 December. Bombs were thrown from adjacent houses as the vehicles were leaving Cork Military Barracks.

Refused to co-operate

James Walsh, Carrick-on-Barrow, County Wexford, farmer and merchant, was shot dead in his shop on 20 December when he refused to co-operate with armed men who were preparing to attack the police barracks across the road. The attack was aborted after the shooting.

Ex-soldier

James Baigriffe (45), an ex-soldier, was found shot dead at Ballykerran, Athlone, on 31 December. A piece of cardboard with the word 'spy' was pinned to his coat.

He worked as a postman until 1914 when he joined the British Army. When he came home from the war he worked as a labourer. He left a wife and three children.

Advice

Dr Gilmartin, Archbishop of Tuam, in his sermon in Tuam Cathedral on Christmas Day, said that although the power to govern came from God, the people have a right for just reasons to seek a change of government. There are two ways of bringing about this change: one by revolution and the other by constitutional action. In the present circumstances of his country, armed resistance to the existing government is unlawful. Firstly, because there is no chance of success, and, secondly, because the evils of such a course would be much greater than the evils it would try to remedy.

Contemporary painting of the Ballyturin ambush in which Mrs Eliza Blake, who was heavily pregnant, was shot dead.

1921

Corner boy

On 5 January, the IRA in Kilkenny shot dead Michael 'Mickey' Cassidy. Cassidy was convicted of being a spy because he used to stand along with other corner boys on Dysart Bridge and chat to soldiers when they passed by. It was decided that he was passing on information prejudicial to the IRA. When two IRA men went to arrest him, he resisted with a pitchfork and was killed in the farmhouse where he was staying.

Taxes

At Drumshanbo, Mohill, County Leitrim, a farmer was badly beaten by two men for refusing to pay a 6d in the pound tax 'for the upkeep of the IRA'.

Crossmaglen postman

Patrick Kirke (23), a postman, despite having an RIC escort, was shot nine times in the back, lungs and liver while delivering old age pension money from Crossmaglen to Cullyhanna, County Armagh, on 13 January. A few hours later, a policeman taking part in a search for Kirke was also shot dead.

Listowel

District Inspector Tobias O'Sullivan was shot dead just outside Listowel Barracks, Kerry, at 1.30 pm on 20 January. He left a wife and a young family. His five-year-old son was with him when he was shot.

Armagh bomb

Sergeant Kemp died on 23 January two days after suffering injuries from a bomb which was thrown at him in Market Street, Armagh. A young passerby, Francis Campbell, was also injured.

Shot in bed

Constables M. Quinn and Thomas Heffron were shot dead and Constable R. Gilmartin was wounded in the Railway View Hotel at the corner of Townhall Street and Oxford Street, Belfast, on 26 January. They were all in bed at the time of the attack.

Dublin hotel

William Doran (45), an ex-serviceman, was shot dead in the Wicklow Hotel in Dublin on 29 January. He worked in the hotel as head porter. He left a wife and family.

Crossfire casualties

Miss Mary Flinten (21) and Thomas Ivery (14) were seriously wounded in crossfire when an Auxiliary armoured tender was fired on in North Earl Street, Dublin. One of the Auxiliary cadets was wounded.

Civilian killed

On 1 February there was an unsuccessful attempt to ambush a military car in Nassau Street, Dublin. One civilian was killed.

Mallow gun-battle

RIC County Inspector Captain King and his wife were fired on near Mallow Railway Station, County Cork, on 31 January. They were both wounded and Mrs Alice King, aged forty, died later. As the ambushers were making their getaway, there was a gun-battle with some RIC policemen who were nearby. Three men who were working in the railway yard at the time were killed and six others wounded by Black and Tans and Auxiliaries.

Court-Martialled

Thomas Bradfield, a Protestant farmer, aged about fifty seven, of Knockmacool House, Desertserges, County Cork, was found shot dead on 2 February at Castlederry, six miles from his residence, with bullet wounds to the heart. A note attached to his clothing said that he had been tried by court martial, found guilty of attempting to give information to the enemy and sentenced to be shot.

Another Thomas Bradfield, a cousin of the first, was shot dead near Bantry, County Cork, by six men on the same night. A piece of cardboard with the word 'spy' was pinned on to his coat.

Miltown JP

At 12.30 am on 2 February, two armed and masked men visited the house of Justice of the Peace Robert Dixon, Miltown, Dunlavin, County Wicklow, and demanded money. When resistance was offered, Dixon was shot dead and his son was seriously wounded.

Surrendered and shot

Two police cars were ambushed at Drumkeen, three miles from New Pallas, County Limerick, at 2.30 pm on 2 February. Eleven policemen were killed. The lorry had been surrounded by armed men who ordered the police to surrender. When they did so they were shot. There were two survivors, District Inspector Samson and a constable.

Torytop

The body of a man (aged about twenty six), shot through the head, was found at Torytop Lane on the outskirts of Cork city on 2 February. There was a piece of paper pinned to his clothing bearing the words, 'Convicted spy. Penalty death. Spies and traitors beware!'

'That's him!'

Corporal John Ryan, a military foot policeman, was shot dead in a licensed house in Old Gloucester Place, Dublin, shortly after 10 am on Saturday, 5 February. He had called for drinks for himself and his brother-in-law, who accompanied him, and while he was reading the morning paper, the *Early Bird*, three men entered the shop, and one was heard to say, 'That's him!' and 'Hands up!' Before the order 'Hands up' could be complied with shots rang out, and Ryan fell, bleeding from wounds to his head and chest. The men then calmly walked away. According to IRA Volunteer Tod Andrews, later, Ryan's last words were, 'What the fuck?'

Enniscorthy execution

On 19 December 1920, Frederick Newsome (21), an ex-soldier, had been shot at in Market Square, Enniscorthy, but escaped injury. At about 9.30 pm on 8 February, Newsome was shot as he crossed over a bridge in Enniscorthy. As he lay on the ground, wounded, one of his two attackers walked up to him and shot him dead. The two men calmly walked away. A man in the company of Newsome was uninjured.

Director

Mr Alfred Reilly, managing director of F. H. Thompson's, bakers and confectioners, Cork, was shot dead when returning home from work on 9 February. His family went to look for him when his pony arrived at his house without him. Not too far from the house they found his body riddled with bullets in the middle of the road. A note pinned to his body said, 'Spy. By order of the IRA, take warning.'

Trench

On the afternoon of 7 February, Patrick Falsey, Kilmacduane, Kilrush, was filling in a trench which had been dug in the road near his house when he was fired on by a number of men. He died at 3 am on 9 February.

Youghal

Alfred Kidney (25), a locksmith, died a week after being shot in the back by three gunmen in Youghal, County Cork, on 3 February. A spent revolver bullet was found in the street after the shooting. Kidney had been physically deformed since birth and could walk only with difficulty. An attempt was made to abduct him the previous October, as he was suspected of giving information to the military but, owing to the resistance he offered, the attempt on that occasion had failed.

Informer

On 11 February, Robert Eady (40), a labourer of Cloghea, Clonakilty, County Cork, was found dead half a mile from his house with bullet wounds to the body and head. It was stated that he had been taken out of his house by armed men and shot. A label pinned to his back bore the words, 'Spies and informers beware!' He left a wife and four children.

Merrion Gate

In an attack on a military lorry at Merrion Gate, Dublin, on Saturday night, 12 February, James Brophy, aged forty-five, was fatally shot in the abdomen while in bed at his residence at 244 Langford Terrace, Merrion Road. Another man, John Healy, aged fifty, was shot dead while walking home in the vicinity of Elm Park. Neither man had anything to do with the military.

Upton Station

On 15 February, the 9.30 am train from Cork to Bantry, containing a small party of troops and a number of civilians, was heavily fired on as it arrived at Upton Station. The troops left their carriage and fired on the attackers who fled, leaving two of their number dead. The fire of the attackers

The cover of an Italian magazine from 1921 that
reported on the Upton ambush.

resulted in the deaths of one woman and six men, one of
them elderly, the wounding of two women and six of the
soldiers who were travelling on the train.

Associate

The body of a man found in a suburb of Cork city on 15
February indicated he had been shot four times. A piece of
cardboard tied around his neck bore the words, 'Convicted

spy. The penalty for all who associate with the Auxiliary cadets, Black and Tans and the RIC - The IRA. P.S. Beware!' He was identified as Mr James Beale, the manager of a large shop in Cork city.

Grave warning

The body of William Sullivan, an ex-soldier, was found near St Joseph's Cemetery, Cork, on 14 February. A card pinned to his chest said that he had been shot as a spy.

Hospital raid

About 7.30 pm on 18 February, six or seven armed men made the porter at Cork Union Workhouse take them to the hospital and then made a wardman show them to St Francis's Ward, where an inmate named Michael Walsh was taken out of bed and told to dress. The party then took Walsh outside and, shortly afterwards, shots were heard. The body of Walsh was found on the roadside with a card bearing the words, 'Caught at last. Spies and informers beware!'

Infirmary

William Mohally, a former recruiting sergeant and a loyalist, was shot and wounded on 19 February in Cork North

District. He was moved to the infirmary. On the morning of 20 February, four armed men entered the infirmary and put Mohally on a stretcher. Mohally was still unconscious at this stage. They took him out into the street and shot him dead. When Mohally was taken outside the hospital, one of the men bent over him, placed a revolver to his mouth and fired. One of the other men said, 'Give him another' and a second bullet was sent through Mohally's cheek. The party then withdrew. Mohally was aged about forty.

Lissanbig landowners

When Matthew Sweetman of Lissanbig, near Skibbereen, County Cork, answered a knock on his door on 19 February he was shot and wounded. Covered in blood, he rushed back into the house and fell. One of the attackers ran inside and shot him in front of his wife and daughters.
William Connell, also of Lissanbig near Skibbereen, heard a knock on his door on the same night. The family were in bed at the time. When the knock came his wife was suspicious, so she got up out of bed and went downstairs to answer the door. When she got there she found that the men had broken in the kitchen door. One of the men held her while the rest ran upstairs. In a few minutes she heard shots and the men came back down. One of them said, 'It is

alright.' All the men then left. Mrs Connell ran upstairs and found her husband lying dead across the bed. He had been shot eight times.

The two men were well-known and extensive farmers. At Pro-Cathedral, Skibbereen, the following Sunday, Reverend F. McCarthy CC strongly condemned the killers.

Ordered to leave

Michael Ryan (35), a labourer, was found shot dead on Saturday morning, 19 February, on the road between Thomaslown and Kilfeakle, about five miles from Tipperary town. He had been warned by the IRA to leave the district. He was a local man and single.

IRA plans for Britain

Sir Hamar Greenwood, the British Government's Chief Secretary for Ireland, in a House of Commons debate on Ireland, quoted from an IRA document captured in raids on the headquarters of the IRA on Saturday, 19 February. Greenwood claimed that the document, under the heading 'Operations Abroad', said:

'Large-scale operations are of paramount importance. I fear, however, that the Volunteers abroad cannot be relied on a large scale with success owing to lack of training. Liverpool

Company gives the greatest hope; Manchester is hopeless; London could do something on a small scale. I have no knowledge of Glasgow, but from the reports which have been received it is clear that they have military instincts and apparently no training. There are possibilities of two large companies in Newcastle-on-Tyne.

'Minor operations could well be carried out in Liverpool, London and possibly Glasgow and Newcastle. The following operations are some that can be carried out, but obviously will require a considerable amount of preparation: the destruction of large ships and buildings by fire, and blast furnaces, possibly the destruction of the coal mines of the district and the destruction of the telegraph and telephone systems of the district, the signalling system, the wrecking of trains and the destruction by fire of crops.

'The officer in charge of operations abroad should be given a free hand. A considerable amount more could be done in Liverpool were he allowed a freer hand. His instructions were to carry out those operations in a way which would cause the least amount of unemployment, exactly the opposite to what is required, particularly at the present moment.

'Operations also should be directed in such channels as would encourage direct action by such bodies as communists and the unemployed acting also with the mob in the direction of looting. Further, the officer in charge should not be tied down by instructions to sparing the life of enemy subjects. For instance, if one train were wrecked it should have the effect of causing considerable alarm to the travelling public and extra expenditure to the railway companies by patrolling the line and providing pilot engines. Also, if gas works were blown up, no doubt lives would be lost, but it would have the effect of throwing the town into darkness and encourage looting.'

The IRA in Britain

British interference in Irish affairs has often led to retaliatory or reprisal actions in Britain. During the rescue of two Irish-American Fenians in Manchester in 1867, IRB Volunteers failed to open a prison van using explosives. Using a gun they then fired at a lock on the van door which ricocheted, killing a Manchester City policeman. Three IRB Volunteers were later hanged for their part in the operation.

Arson attack, Liverpool, December 1920

Later that year there was another IRB attempt to rescue a prisoner held in London's Clerkenwell Prison using a barrel of gunpowder. It exploded, killing twelve civilians and injuring one hundred and twenty others.

O'Donovan Rossa had been sentenced to natural life in jail in England for high treason in 1865. He was later released as part of an amnesty which included banishment to North America. From there he advocated dynamite attacks on English cities. The attacks between 1881 and 1885 targeted military barracks in Salford (in which a seven-year-old boy was killed) and Chester, a police station in Liverpool, London's Mansion House, Victoria Station, Charing Cross Station, Ludgate Hill Station, Paddington and Westminster Bridge stations which injured seventy people. Also attacked were the office of *The Times,* the headquarters of the Special Branch, the Palace of Westminster, the Tower of London, with attacks on the Carlton Club, a gentlemen's club for members of the Conservative Party, and the home of Conservative MP Sir Watkin Williams-Wynn. In an explosion at a gasworks in Glasgow, a dozen people were injured. Two IRB Volunteers also lost their lives in a premature explosion.

Among those arrested and sentenced for involvement in the campaign was Thomas Clarke who would be the first signatory of the 1916 Proclamation.

Despite the thousands of Irish who had laid down their lives fighting in World War One, the British Government in March 1918 announced plans to introduce conscription in Ireland. The threat of forced enlistment created widespread anger (and opposition from the Catholic Church hierarchy). Cathal Brugha organised an eleven-man squad to assassinate British Government ministers from the public gallery of the House of Commons should they pass a Conscription Bill. Volunteers closely monitored the movements of ministers, including Bonar Law, and reconnoitred the home of Lloyd George in Wales. The Volunteers were withdrawn only because of the change in Britain's fortunes at the Western Front and when the threat of conscription was lifted.

On the morning of attacks on intelligence officers in Dublin in November 1920, the IRA's plans for simultaneous attacks on large-scale commercial targets in England, including sabotage and arson attacks on Liverpool docks and the destruction of a power plant, had to be abandoned after the capture of documents.

The IRA was to carry out almost two hundred and forty attacks in Britain against power-stations and water-works, warehouses, hotels and cafes. There were also shooting incidents between Volunteers and police, usually in pursuit of suspects. In November, the IRA killed a nineteen-year-old civilian, William Ward, who gave chase. In St Albans they shot an Auxiliary and his wife, and attacked the homes of Auxiliaries, including those of their relatives. They laid siege to the home of a councillor, John Rimmer (who had earlier interfered with an operation), setting fire to his farm building and shooting through his windows. One of those involved, Edward Brady, later said, 'It was terrible but it was all part of the war in the struggle of a nation to free itself.'

In June 1922, IRA Volunteers under the command of Sam Maguire assassinated Field Marshal Sir Henry Wilson in London. The British threatened that unless the Provisional Government took action they would. And so, at 4.15 am on 28 June, Free State forces attacked the IRA headquarters in the Four Courts, Dublin, triggering the Civil War.

Arms raid

James Toner, a farmer of Lagan, near Keady, County Armagh, died on 20 February as a result of bullet wounds received in an arms raid on 2 February. He was shot as four raiders entered his house looking for arms. They found no weapons and, as they were leaving, they warned the occupants of the house not to leave for an hour.

Kidnapped

Constable Frederick W. Perrier was shot dead and Constable P. G. Kerins was seriously wounded when they were attacked by a party of armed men in Bandon, County Cork, on 23 February. The attackers then kidnapped two unarmed soldiers and two naval wireless men who were talking to some girls. The wireless men were soon released but the two soldiers, Lance-Corporal Stubbs and Private Knight, were taken to a suburb of the town and shot dead.

Cadets

A large party of Auxiliary cadets was ambushed on the Macroom to Ballyvourney Road on 25 February. Major C. V. Grant MC, the leader of the party, and Constable Arthur Cane were killed, five cadets were wounded and one RIC driver was seriously wounded.

Lamp Post Notice

An ex-soldier, Henry Murray from Dooragh outside Carrickmacross, County Monaghan, was shot dead in Chapel Street, Dundalk, about 7 pm on 25 February. Notices were fixed to nearby lamp posts stating that Murray had been tried and convicted as a spy and informer by the IRA and executed.

Collections

Three houses in the same area of County Tipperary were visited by armed and masked men collecting funds for the IRA in late February. When they were refused admission to one of these houses, stones were thrown through the windows and abuse was shouted at the occupants. They then forced their way into a second house and tried to carry off a safe but found it was too heavy. At the third house, the men just left on being refused admission again.

Strollers

A number of armed IRA men attacked a party of unarmed and off-duty soldiers who were out for a walk in the streets of Cork at 10.30 pm on 28 February. Six of the soldiers were killed and twelve were injured. Five of the dead were aged twenty.

Convicted

Thomas Cotter, a civilian, was shot dead on 1 March when he answered his front door. A card attached to his body read, 'Convicted spy—IRA.'

Bad company

In early March, police found posted on a telegraph pole in the vicinity of Mountmellick, County Laois, a notice which stated: 'Final warning. Information has been received by our Secret Service that certain females in this district are known to be keeping company with enemy Black and Tans and RIC. We give this, our final warning, that unless this conduct ceases they may be prepared to suffer the consequences.—O/C.'

Special brother

The home of Lily Stitt at Parker Street, off the Newtownards Road, Belfast, was raided by armed men on 3 March. The men were looking for her brother, who was a Special Constable stationed at a country barracks. When they realised he wasn't there, they tied Lily to a chair, cropped her hair and stole £4 from her.

Blacknell

Frank Elliott, an ex-serviceman, was taken from his house, where he lived with his wife and four children, at Blacknell, County Roscommon, by armed men on Thursday night, 3 March. He was walked about two miles by the men before being shot dead.

Pub killing

RIC Constable R. Beasant was shot dead in a public house on Friday night, 4 March, in Cashel, County Tipperary, by two armed men. Miss Josie Cantwell, who was believed to be romantically involved with Beasant, was badly wounded when she was shot in the head.

Mistake

On 6 March, a hired car carrying two passengers was waved down on the Malahide Road, Dublin, before bombs were thrown and shots fired at it. The attackers thought it was carrying British Army officers. The driver, John O'Neill, was killed. When the attackers checked the identities of the passengers they said they had mistaken the vehicle for another.

IRA court

Francis McPhillips, aged about twenty, of Corleek, Latnamarel, Aghabog, County Monaghan, was taken from his house on 9 March, where he lived with his widowed mother and six sisters. His body was found in a hollow some miles away with a card attached to it saying, 'Tried, convicted and executed by the IRA.'

Three weeks earlier he had been held up by four armed men, blindfolded and chained to the gates of Aghabog Church. He was accused of giving information to the police about a man on the run. Another man, Patrick J. Larner of Marnahan, near Rockcorry, County Monaghan, was found in the same hollow. He was aged about thirty and had a card attached to his clothing: 'Tried and convicted informer.'

Executed

James Maher of Thurles and P. Meara, both ex-soldiers, were found shot dead at Ballyranson, Killenaule district, County Tipperary, on 9 March. The word 'spy' was pinned to Meara's breast.

Barracks worker

On Thursday night, 10 March, James Good, who was employed in Cork Military Barracks, was nearing his home in Tower Street when he was fired at. The bullet passed through his shoulder and out of his mouth. He died shortly afterwards. He had received a notice giving him fourteen days to leave Cork. Good was an ex-serviceman and was an extensive farmer.

His son was to be shot dead by masked and armed men three weeks later.

Conversation

Two RIC policemen (from Cornwall and Inverness) were talking to some young women at Victoria Square, Belfast, on 11 March when four or five men from the Belfast Brigade IRA produced revolvers and started firing at them. The two policemen were killed. A civilian who was wounded, Alexander Allen, aged fifty, died the following day, whether from IRA rounds or from one of the mortally wounded policemen is not known.

Disappearance of Mrs Lindsay

A planned IRA ambush on British forces between Dripsey and Coachford, Cork, on 28 January had been compromised and thwarted, leading to the deaths of six Volunteers in total, five by execution on 28 February. The IRA believed that Mrs Mary Lindsay, a widow who lived in Leemont House, Coachford, tipped off the military. She and her driver, James Clarke (50), originally from Banbridge, County Down, were taken from Leemont on 17 February. Her house was then burned down. The IRA offered to exchange their two hostages for the five Volunteers facing death sentences. A letter of appeal, written by Mrs Lindsay, asking for a reprieve for the men, was also delivered to Major-General Strickland of the British Army but was ignored. Sometime between 11 March and 16 March, Mrs Lindsay and James Clarke were taken from the house in which they had been held for over three weeks, shot dead and buried in an unmarked grave in a bog. Their bodies have never been found.

Disappearances

*The authoritarian Richard Mulcahy, doyen of the
Free Staters, was IRA Chief of Staff throughout
the time of most of the Disappearances and leader
of Fine Gael, 1944-59*

Over one hundred people were killed and disappeared by the IRA during the Tan War, sixty-four in County Cork alone, including two women. Almost half the bodies have never been recovered. There is no precise figure for the numbers of persons disappeared. Extensive research has been carried out by historians Pádraig Óg Ó Ruaric, Andy Bielenberg and John Borgonovo, with a figure of 108 disappearances. Professor Eunan O'Halpin suggested a figure of approximately two hundred.

One of those involved in several of the killings and disappearances was Martin Corry, who went on to become a long-serving Fianna Fáil TD. Though IRA veterans and the authorities who were approached by relatives attempted to locate some remains at least seventy bodies were never recovered.

One of those kidnapped, killed and disappeared by Free State forces two months after the Civil War ended was Noel Lemass, brother of a future Taoiseach, Seán Lemass. His mutilated body was found three months later. He had been shot three times, his left arm had been fractured and his right foot was missing.

No similar body to the *Independent Commission for the Location of Victims' Remains* established in 1999 as part of the Good Friday Agreement and with which the Republican Movement liaised and fully cooperated was ever set up by any Irish Government to recover the missing of the Tan War.

In 1990, the body of Thomas Kirby, shot as a spy, was recovered from a Tipperary bog, and in 1998 the body of Patrick Joyce, an informer from Galway, was discovered in Connemara. The remains of nineteen-year-old Private George Chalmers, disappeared in June 1921, were not recovered until May 2018.

Home addresses

Documents recently captured belonging to the IRA (dated 31 January, 1921):

'It has been suggested, and I agree, that all Auxiliary correspondence be seized whenever possible in order that a list be made of their home addresses with a view to further action.'

A letter from GHQ of the IRA, dated 4 January, to the Director of Information of the IRA and initialed by the Chief of Staff, reads:

'1. The English address of General Strickland is required.

'2. By the end of the week it is possible we may require a list of English addresses of Auxiliary police and Black and Tans as far as we have them up to date.'

Attached to this document are lists of private addresses in England such as those of General Strickland and of Auxiliary cadets including that of one called Reynolds, whose farms near Liverpool had been 'mysteriously' burned a short time previously.

Resignations

In parliamentary papers, Sir Hamar Greenwood said that in the twelve months ending 12 February 1921, there had been 2,193 resignations from the RIC and 131 from the Auxiliaries.

Tralee train

The train travelling from Listowel to Tralee on Saturday, 12 March, was fired on by armed men when it pulled into Ardfert Station. An Auxiliary, Walter Falkiner, was shot dead and the train driver, O'Shea, was wounded in the head and hip. A postman travelling on the train had his head grazed by a bullet as the train picked up speed leaving the station.

Sinn Féin magistrate

Thomas Shannon, a farmer of Kilrush, County Clare, was shot dead at his farmhouse door on the evening of 13 March. Official enquiries stated that he was killed soon after an attempt to sever connections with the Sinn Féin movement. Twelve months previously, he had been elected a Sinn Féin magistrate but criticised the methods of the court. He refused to pay rates to a Sinn Féin collector and was shot ten days later.

Pearse Street ambush

A raiding party of Auxiliary police driving in lorries and an armoured car along Great Brunswick Street (now Pearse Street), Dublin, on 14 March, was attacked by Volunteers. Section Leader B. J. L Beard MC and Cadet O'Farrell, an Irishman, were killed by gunfire.

About thirty yards from the shooting, seventy-year-old Mary Morgan was seriously injured and fell to the ground—she died later from her wounds. Stephen Clarke (22), an ex-serviceman, was shot dead as he tried to pick Mrs Morgan up and get her to safety. Thomas Asquith, a caretaker who was standing opposite his house, was also shot dead. His wife had a narrow escape. A member of Sinn Féin and two IRA Volunteers also lost their lives.

Appeal to Dev

Forty-five-year old Bridget Noble, a married woman, who was accused of consorting with the RIC in Castletownbere was kidnapped by the IRA on 4 March and shot dead on 15 March. It is not sure if her body was buried or thrown into the sea. Her husband twice wrote to de Valera appealing for the return of her remains and said, 'It is not clean work to take away my lone and defenceless wife.' There is no record of a reply. Her body was never recovered.

Tailor

A man named Leacock, a tailor, was taken from his work on the evening of 1 March by armed men. His dead body was found riddled with bullets outside Kenagh, County Longford, on Wednesday, 16 March. There was a note attached to his body: 'Shot by IRA for spying and giving information. Other spies take warning.'

Statistics

The following statement was issued to the press by Dublin Castle on 18 March:

'The press has detailed very faithfully the inconvenience to which citizens are being put and the economic losses that are being sustained by traders and others as a result of nine o'clock curfew order which was recently put in force in Dublin in consequence of repeated attacks in the streets of the city by armed civilians upon the forces of the crown.

'The following statistics show further how grave is the danger to the public of these attacks, as compared with their slight measure of success against the crown forces upon whom they are directed.

'Since January 1st 1921, there have been, within the Dublin Metropolitan Police area, 50 attacks on the forces of the crown, resulting in the following casualties:-

Military	1 killed	12 wounded
Police	4 killed	20 wounded
Total	5 killed	32 wounded
Civilians	7 killed	40 wounded

'Owing to the fact that the attackers, to secure their own safety, not only dress in civilian clothes, but also make use of the general public to cover their retreat and even their attack itself, there were among these casualties a considerable proportion of women and children. The loss of life and the wounding of law-abiding and innocent people, the restrictions of public freedom of movement and of trade, are all regrettable, but they are inevitable so long as outrages of this kind continue.'

The Castle added that Michael Collins, Charles Burgess (Cathal Brugha), and Richard Mulcahy were the individuals directly responsible for organising and controlling these ambushes.

Boycott

On Friday night, 18 March, the public in and around Ballybay, County Monaghan, were warned in a circular headed 'IRA', not to enter twenty-three businesses in Ballybay and district that were trading with Belfast, thereby breaking the Belfast boycott that was in operation then. Failure to comply with the order was threatened with action by the IRA. The notice was posted on some farmers' doors and gate entrances.

Shoppers injured
While a military patrol lorry of the South Lancashire
Regiment was proceeding along Aungier Street, Dublin, at
6.35 pm on Saturday, 19 March, three bombs were thrown
at it, followed by a number of shots. Two of the bombs
exploded in the lorry, killing two of the occupants and
wounding six others. Several civilians were detained in
hospital for injuries received during the attack. The street
was crowded with shoppers at the time of the attack.

Sick leave
Constable William Campbell, who was off-duty and on sick
leave, was shot dead at the back of his lodgings at
Mullinahone. County Tipperary, by unknown men on
Saturday, 20 March.

The Headford Ambush
On Monday, 21 March, the IRA ambushed a train carrying
British soldiers near Headford Junction, midway between
Rathmore and Killarney, County Kerry. They were
commanded by Tom McEllistrim (who was later a Fianna
Fáil TD for over forty years). One officer and eight other
ranks were killed and ten other ranks wounded. Three

civilians also lost their lives: John Breen, Michael Cagney and Patrick O'Donoghue.

Summonsed

Martin Daly, aged sixty, was shot dead on 21 March near Tralee, County Kerry. He had been living in fear of his life ever since he handed a Sinn Féin summons over to the military. He was blindfolded and his hands were tied behind his back before being shot. Medical evidence showed that there were numerous injuries to the body. The face was peppered with small-shot and his jaw was broken. Some ribs were broken and a shot had passed through his lungs. A notice was found on the breast of his coat which read, 'Informers beware! Convicted informer.'

Booladurragh

At Booladurragh, about six miles from Enniscorthy, County Wexford, James Skelton (21), an ex-soldier, and his brother John (25) were both shot dead on 21 March. James had a handkerchief partly tied about his face and a card on his neck with the words, 'Convicted spy—IRA.' There was also a card around John's neck: 'Let all spies beware. On your track—Flying Column, IRA.'

Twelve-year-old killed

On 24 March, Denis Lenehan, a former sergeant-major of
the Leinster Regiment, was walking along Cork Street,
Dublin, when three unknown men rushed from a gateway
and opened fire on him with revolvers, wounding him in
several places. A twelve-year-old girl, Hannah Keegan, was
shot dead and another young girl was wounded, as was a
man named Brady who was walking by at the time. Lenehan
used to be employed in Ballykinlar Camp, County Down,
and had been transferred to Islandbridge Barracks.

Good Friday killing

Mr John Cathcart, managing director of Paisley & Co Ltd, a
widower with three children, was shot dead at his house in
Pearce's Square, Youghal, County Cork, on 25 March by
armed raiders who forcibly entered his house at the back. An
envelope with the words, 'Convicted spy. Spies and
informers beware—IRA,' was found near the body. The
raiders said that they were looking for arms. When Cathcart
told them he had none, he was shot four times.

Unknown man

An unknown man, aged about thirty, was found shot dead
near Kenmare, County Kerry. He was blindfolded, his hands

were tied behind his back and there was a card attached to him bearing the words, 'Spies beware—IRA.'

Son shot

Mr William Good of Barryshall, Timoleague, County Cork, was taken off his pony and trap by armed men and shot dead on the roadside returning from Bandon on Saturday evening, 26 March. On his body was a note with the words, 'Tried, convicted and executed. Spies and informers beware—IRA.'

William Good's father, James Good, had been shot dead by masked men three weeks previously, on 10 March, at his own door. William Good Jnr was at home from Trinity College since his father's death.

Schoolteacher

John Brosnan (18), schoolteacher, was walking along Bridge Street, Tralee, when the IRA threw a Mills bomb at three policemen in a car. The grenade bounced off the car and exploded, mortally wounding the teacher—who would die from his wounds eight days later—and injuring two other passers-by.

Telephone exchange

As part of its campaign to destroy communications, the IRA set fire to a local telephone exchange in Killiney, Dublin, above which lived the Fitzhughs, a family of eleven. Thirteen-year-old Thomas Fitzhugh was killed and several others received burns before escaping the flames.

Sisters

Kate Burke was killed and her sister, Mamie Burke, was injured during a grenade attack on a passing military lorry in Amiens Street, Dublin, on Tuesday, 29 March. Kate was standing in Amiens Street, waiting for her sister who worked in the post office, when she was seriously wounded in the forehead and abdomen by the exploding bomb.

Engaged

Captain Cecil Lees, aged about forty-four, was shot dead just after leaving St Andrew's Hotel in Exchequer Street, Dublin, on Tuesday, 29 March. He had been employed for some time on government clerical work in Dublin and had only recently become engaged to be married.

Protestant farmer

William Fleming, a Protestant farmer of Drumgarra, County Monaghan, was called on by armed and masked men who demanded his gun on Tuesday, 29 March. The Flemings refused to hand over anything and the men set fire to their house. Fleming and his son, Robert, were taken to the main road and shot dead. Up to forty people were supposed to be involved. William Fleming's mother, aged eighty, and her grandchildren, aged nine and eleven, were present at the time of the attack.

There had been a raid for arms at the house the previous September. On that occasion, a member of the attacking party was shot dead and William Fleming was wounded. Mrs Fleming and the two grandchildren had to move to the Castleblayney Workhouse because of the destruction of their home.

Appeal

The Archbishop of Tuam issued an appeal for a 'truce of God':

'I appeal to the young men of this diocese to continue to abstain from deeds of blood, no matter what the provocation. I appeal to them to imitate the patience of Christ, who was led like, as a lamb to the slaughter, the victim of wickedness, but who, when all was darkest, arose in the power of immortality.'

Navy pensioner

Denis Donovan, was a postman in Bandon, insurance agent and a naval pensioner with twenty-three years' service. He was shot dead by armed men outside his home on Tuesday evening, 29 March, after a caller asked his wife, 'Is Denis inside? I want to see him about some insurance.' Donovan left a wife and three children.

Roscarberry raid

Roscarberry Barracks, County Cork, was attacked on 30 March. Bombs were first thrown and then the attackers opened up with guns. Sergeant O'Shea and Constables Bowles and Reynolds were killed. Nine police were wounded.

The following day, a child found an unexploded Mills grenade at the scene and gave it to an RIC man who threw it against a wall. It exploded killing two local farmers and wounding several bystanders. Four-year-old Cornelius Fitzpatrick also died two days later from shrapnel fragments.

Agent in England

A man was found shot dead on the golf links at Ashford, Middlesex, England, on 3 April. He had a bullet wound in the chest. On a piece of paper found near the body were the words, 'Let spies and traitors beware—IRA.' He was identified as twenty-year-old Vincent Fovargue of 20 Dunville Road, Ranelagh, Dublin, a former IRA Volunteer suspected of informing. His family strongly and persistently denied that he was a spy. His mother said: 'We knew better than anyone else what kind of boy he was. I also wish it to be understood that I do not for an instant blame the IRA for his murder.'

Fovargue had been arrested by the British in Rathmines on 4 January. He fled from a military lorry taking him to Kilmainham during a bogus ambush on the convoy at the end of January and which the IRA believed was staged to facilitate his escape. He then left the country on the advice of his family. He used the name Staunton as an alias when in England. Fovargue's name appears on the list of executions by the IRA.

Former fusilier

Thomas Morris (68), who served in the Royal Irish Fusiliers during World War One and had been in the Royal Irish

Constabulary for fourteen years, was taken from his home near Kinvarra, County Galway, on Saturday night, 2 April, and was found shot dead, probably from a shotgun blast to the chest, the following morning. He had been blindfolded and labelled. 'Convicted spy. Tried, convicted and executed—IRA.'

Killeshandra

RIC Constable James Duffy and a civilian were attacked on Sunday night, 3 April, near Killeshandra, County Cavan. The civilian, Henry James, was wounded. Duffy was captured and taken over a mile away before being shot dead. There were a large number of bullet wounds in the body.

Water supply

An unsuccessful attempt, attributed to 'Sinn Féiners', was made to blow up the Thirlmere pipe conveying the Manchester water supply at Agecroft Bridge, Pendlebury, on 4 April.

Dead dogs

A notice was displayed in different parts of the country containing words of warning to anyone owning dogs: 'These people are warned not to pay licence to the enemy, and those who do so will have their dogs shot dead and the persons themselves will be severely dealt with.' The notice was signed, 'By order of the IRA.'

Assisted wounded policemen
Edward Beirne (50), a farmer from Scramogue, two miles from Strokestown, County Roscommon, was taken from his house by twenty armed men on the night of 5 April and shot dead. There was a label attached to his body with the words, 'Convicted spy. Spies and informers beware of the Flying Column.' He was an opponent of Sinn Féin and had assisted wounded policemen at the scene of an ambush.

Shoemaker
The dead body of an ex-soldier named John O'Mahony, better known as 'Boxer' O'Mahony, was found with three bullet wounds in his head at Borleen, Rahounane, on the north side of Tralee, County Kerry, on 6 April. O'Mahony, a shoemaker, was a widower with nine children, was taken out of Rourke's pub, questioned and then sentenced to death. A note pinned to his body read, 'Convicted spy. Traitors beware!'

Ranger

Former Connaught Ranger John Gilligan (40) and John Wymes (66), who had been dismissed from the RIC in 1901, were taken from their homes and shot dead in separate incidents at Loughglynn, in the Castlerea district of County Roscommon, on 8 April. They were both accused of being informers.

Thrown into the Shannon

After court-martialling as an alleged spy John McNamee from Drumlish, County Longford, a married, family man, the IRA threw his body into the River Shannon. They later claimed it was thrown into the Shannon with the aim of saving his children from disgrace and shame.

Castlerea

Ed Weldon (20), a lance corporal in the Leicestershire Regiment, was fatally shot twice in the chest when stopped by an IRA Volunteer asking for a light in Main Street around 10.15 on the night of 8 April. More shots were fired at soldiers at the scene, killing Mary Ann McDonagh (60), wife of a publican, and wounding civilian Peter Noone in the right leg.

Crossmaglen attack

Constable John Fluke (28) of the Ulster Special Constabulary (formed in November 1920 mainly of members of the Ulster Volunteer Force) was killed and Constables Dougal, Hands and Linton were wounded when a bomb was thrown and shots fired at them on 10 April. They had been on their way to service in Creggan Church, a couple of miles outside Crossmaglen but came across an IRA operation. Constable Fluke's wife was pregnant with the couple's first child.

Limerick

An RIC patrol was attacked in John's Street, Limerick, on the evening of Friday, 8 April. A Head Constable, two sergeants and a constable were seriously wounded when bombs were thrown at them. One of the bombs landed in the front window of the home of Francis McMahon (65), a civilian, killing him instantly. Another three civilians were hurt by shrapnel. Shortly afterwards, an unarmed member of the RIC, Constable Hugh Wiggins (27), was talking to a woman in John's Square when he was surprised by a group of IRA Volunteers who shot him. He died the following day.

In his dressing gown

The IRA, in one of many raids and arson attacks on 'Big

Houses'—two hundred and seventy-five in total were destroyed—to prevent them being occupied as barracks by the British Army, raided Kilmorna House, Listowel, Kerry, the home of Sir Arthur Vicars, on the night of 14 April. They took the fifty-seven-year-old, who was in his dressing gown, outside to the lawn where they shot him dead, leaving a notice which read, 'Traitors beware! We do not forget—IRA.' Vicars had entertained British soldiers at his house. A week earlier, during an attack on soldiers leaving the estate, IRA Volunteer Michael Galvin had been shot and killed.

The IRA claimed that Vicars was armed with a revolver and attempted to flee, something denied by his valet. Vicars was formerly 'Ulster King of Arms' and was custodian of the Irish Crown Jewels in Dublin Castle until 1907, when they were stolen—and never recovered. Vicars was a half-brother of Pierce O'Mahony, who was for several years a prominent member of Parnell's Irish Parliamentary Party and who stuck with Parnell at the time of a split in the party thirty years previously.

Local people had thought Vicars 'a decent, if eccentric, gentleman'.

After shooting him, the IRA set the house on fire, completely destroying it.

Farmhouse

John McCabe, an ex-soldier living in Crossmaglen, County Armagh, was found shot in a stable at a farmhouse near Carrickmacross, County Monaghan. His hands were tied with his belt and his clothing was saturated with blood. He had been shot four times and a card pinned to his clothing read, 'Convicted spy—IRA.' McCabe, although badly wounded, had managed to escape from his captors and made his way to the farmhouse in the early hours of the morning but was unable to waken anybody so he went into the stable where he was found later.

Girlfriend

Between 8 pm and 9 pm on Friday, 15 April, while Constable Wilfred Jones, an Englishman stationed at Ballinamore RIC Barracks, was leaving home his girlfriend, Miss Margaret Sadlier, a postal official in the local post office, he was fired on at the railway station. He returned the fire but he was shot dead through the heart. Miss Sadlier was seriously wounded.

Hair

On the night of 16 April, a number of armed and masked men visited the house of Mary Gallagher, aged fifty-six, of

Derrybeg, and cut off her hair, apparently because she had reported a neighbour to the crown forces for 'having poisoned her dog'.

Pub bomb

At 10.45 pm on Saturday, 16 April, at Ennis, County Clare, a small party of armed men threw a hand grenade and fired revolver shots into Shaughnessy's public house, killing Royal Scots Sergeant Sidney Rew. Kate Shaughnessy, the proprietor, and a Mrs Gallagher from Limerick were seriously wounded.

'A real soldier'

Major Geoffrey Lee Compton-Smith, Royal Welch Fusiliers, was in civilian clothes and out buying cigarettes and a newspaper in a shop in Blarney, County Cork, on 16 April, when he was picked up by the IRA and brought to a place they called 'The Cottage', where fifteen others had been executed. They offered to exchange him for Volunteers facing execution but the exchange was refused. Compton-Smith reportedly accepted his death sentence, leaving his watch to the senior IRA officer in charge whom he considered to be carrying out his duty. He wrote to his wife; 'I intend to die like a Welch fusilier with a laugh and forgiveness for those who are carrying out the deed … [I have] learned to regard Sinn Féiners as mistaken idealists than as a "Murder Gang".' One of the Volunteers described him as 'a real soldier'.

His body was buried in a bog in Donoughmore from where it was recovered five years later.

Woman executed

A single woman named Kathleen Carroll (36) was shot dead in the early hours of Sunday morning, 17 April. She was taken from her house at Aughnamena, near Duffy's Cross, about six miles from Monaghan town. A party of armed and masked men forced their way into the house where she lived with her aged mother and middle-aged brother. They tied her hands behind her back and took her out of the house. She was made to walk a mile before being shot dead in a laneway. On a label attached to her clothing was written, 'Tried, convicted and executed by the IRA. Spies and informers beware!'

Miss Carroll had written some letters to the police concerning illicit drink trafficking in the district and the movements of IRA Volunteers. These letters were captured by the IRA and it was thought that this was the reason for her killing. As Kathleen Carroll was being dragged away, one of the men was heard to say to her that she would tell the police nothing more about the stills in that area. Her name appears on the list of executions claimed by the IRA.

Last rites

John O'Reilly (40), an ex-soldier of Newmarket-on-Fergus, County Clare, was taken from his house by armed men on 20 April and shot dead in the road at Ballycar, two miles from his home.

O'Reilly was shot in the presence of a priest who was taken there to administer the last rites. A notice was pinned on the dead man's coat: 'Spy. Executed by IRA. Getting them at last. Beware!'

Castle review

The weekly review of Irish conditions issued from Dublin Castle state the following up to 16 April:

Courthouses destroyed	74
Police barracks destroyed	538
Police barracks damaged	250
Raids for arms	3,111
Policemen killed	281
Policemen wounded	455
Soldiers killed	281
Soldiers wounded	219

Casualties

Total casualties to crown forces and civilians in Ireland from 16-23 April: nineteen police and two military killed; twenty-six police and eleven military wounded. Civilian casualties, including republicans: twenty-seven killed and thirty-two wounded.

Donegall Place, Belfast

Two Auxiliary cadets had been on escort duty to Belfast and were due to return to Sligo on Saturday evening, 23 April, when their train was delayed. Spotted by the IRA, they were shot. One died immediately, the other the following day.

Oughterard

A police patrol from Oughterard, County Galway, was ambushed at Kilmilkin on Sunday, 24 April. Constable John Boylan was killed and Sergeant Hanley and Constable Rutledge were seriously wounded. Boylan was a widower with five young children. Father Cunningham, the Catholic curate for Lehane who drove to the scene, was fired on while attending to the wounded police.

Hostage

Gilbert M. Potter (43), a District Inspector in the RIC, was kidnapped while driving by car to Cahir, County Tipperary. He was fired upon by a number of armed men who rendered the car useless and captured him. Potter was held prisoner for several days by the IRA. The IRA made an offer to exchange him for an IRA prisoner, Thomas Traynor, who was under sentence of death. When Traynor was hanged, Potter was shot dead.

Schoolchildren

Children going to school at Clonbern, Tuam district, on 27 April, found the dead body of Thomas Hanna on the roadside. He had been shot. On a piece of paper pinned to his coat were the words, 'Convicted spy—Executed by IRA.'

Survived

District Inspector Ferris, transferred from Cork and believed to have been involved in the assassination of Tomás MacCurtain in the city, was shot by the IRA after he left St Paul's Parochial House on the Falls Road, Belfast. Despite being wounded in the head, neck and abdomen he survived.

Tourmakeady

Five policemen were killed in an ambush at Tourmakeady, County Mayo, on 3 May. They were Sergeant Creggan and Constables Oakes, Flynn, Power and O'Regan. An IRA prisoner, Patrick Feeney, was shot dead by British soldiers, and another Volunteer, Michel O'Brien, was killed in a shoot-out during the retreat.

Eight RIC police killed

Eight RIC policemen were killed in an ambush near the village of Rathmore on the Cork/Kerry border on 4 May. The police patrol (one sergeant and eight constables) left the barracks at Rathmore to look for a reported dead body with a 'spy' label attached when they were attacked. The dead men were Sergeant Thomas McCormack and Constables James Phelan, Alfred Hillan, Samuel Watkin, Walter T. Brown, William A. Clomp, Robert Dyne and H.B. Woodcock; Constable Hickey escaped.

The attackers had killed an eighty-year-old man, 'Old Tom' (Thomas) O'Sullivan, who had been seen meeting the Black and Tans in Killarney Barracks, and left him on the Bog Road. They pinned a 'spy note' to his body, and used his body as bait for the ambush. It was strongly denied that he was a spy. It was said that he had no connection or association with the police or military. His son was killed in World War One and he drew a pension on that.

Dragged from their beds

Martin Scanlon, an RIC pensioner, and John McAuley, a sub-postmaster, were dragged from their beds near Kilrooskey, County Roscommon, on 9 May and shot as spies by the IRA. Their bodies, riddled with bullets, were found close together about two miles from McAuley's house. Both had labels attached: 'Convicted spy. Tried by IRA.' Scanlon left a widow and four children.

A woman accused of supplying the police with milk in County Roscommon had pig rings clamped to her buttocks with pincers.

Hen House Killing

RIC Constables Alexander Clarke and Charles Murdoch left their barracks in Clonmany, County Donegal and went for a walk around 7 pm on 9 May. They were attacked and shot by IRA Volunteers and thrown into the sea. Clarke drowned but Murdock managed to swim back to shore at Binnion. He sought refuge in a house but the locals turned him over to the IRA. He was finished off in the hen house with a hatchet and was later secretly buried either on a local strand or near the town cemetery, his body never being recovered.

Grafton Street

Fourteen civilians, including a number of women and a boy, were injured when bombs were thrown at tenders containing Auxiliaries in Grafton Street, Dublin, on 12 May. None of the Auxiliaries was injured. They did not return fire. The Auxiliaries supplied medical treatment to the civilians, some of whom were very seriously injured.

District inspector

RIC District Inspector Biggs and Miss Winifred Barrington were shot dead on 14 May when their car was attacked between Glenstal and Newport, County Limerick, after visiting the home of Major Gabbit. Three other passengers, including a woman, escaped. Gabbit jumped from the car, shouting that there were women on board. Winifred Barrington, aged twenty three, was the only daughter of Sir Charles Barrington of Glenstal Castle. During a shouting match following the killings, one of the IRA men was reported as saying, 'Only for the bitch being in bad company she would not have been shot.'

Soccer

At Bandon, on 14 May, Francis Shepherd (19) of the Essex Regiment, who was protecting police and soldiers playing football in the grounds of a grammar school next to the barracks, was shot dead. Two civilians were wounded. One of them, Cornelius Looney, an elderly man, died later that night.

Pub and parochial house

RIC Sergeant Joseph Coleman was shot dead through the window of a pub in Midleton, Cork, on 14 May. His colleagues went to get a priest but were attacked again by the IRA outside the parochial house. Here, Constables Thoman Cornyan and Harold Thompson were shot dead.

Lured by young women

On 14 May, a group of soldiers from the King's Own Scottish Borderers left their camp in Castletownbere, County Cork, for a walk, apparently lured out by three young women who encouraged the soldiers to follow them to a local waterfall. After going about three miles the girls disappeared and the soldiers, who were unarmed, were met on the seashore by a large number of IRA men. One soldier escaped by swimming out to sea while another ran to safety in the mountains. The remaining four were placed with their backs to a ditch and fired on repeatedly. Three of them died. They were: Private J. Hunter, Bridgeton, Glasgow; Private Donal Chambers, Lower Sydenham, London; and Private Robert McMullin, Rutherglen, Glasgow. Before he died, McMullen pleaded, 'You want to play the game, Mac.'

Chapel

At 10.50 am on 15 May, three RIC policemen were fired on as they were leaving Mass in Bansha, Tipperary. Constable John Nutley was killed, Sergeant Jeremiah Sullivan seriously wounded and the other constable slightly wounded.

Heavily pregnant

On Sunday evening, 15 May, Captain and RIC District Inspector C. E. M. Blake, who had been stationed at Gort, County Galway, since November 1920, Mrs Eliza Blake, his heavily pregnant wife, Captain Fiennes Cornwallis of the 17th Lancers and Lieutenant Robert McCreery of the same regiment were all shot dead after leaving a tennis party at Ballyturin House, about four miles from Gort. Lily Gregory, daughter-in-law of Lady Augusta Gregory, was the sole survivor. Police, soldiers and a doctor were fired on as they arrived at the scene—Constable John Kearney died from gunshot wounds on 21 May. Among the attackers was Patrick Glynn who in 1927 became a Fianna Fáil TD.

Killiney Links
Peter Graham, who worked at the Pavilion Garden at
Killiney Golf Links, was found shot dead near the golf links
on Sunday, 15 May. He had a label attached to his body:
'Convicted spy. Tried and found guilty by the IRA.' He had
five bullet wounds to the head.

Highest casualties since 1916
According to the Dublin Castle weekly review of conditions
in Ireland, the number of police and military casualties in
Ireland for the week that ended 16 May was the highest
since 1916. They numbered fifty-five, including twenty-
three deaths. Nearly half of these casualties, says the Castle
review, occurred on 14 May, the day following the elections
for the Southern parliament, and there seems no doubt that
they were the outcome of a prearranged plan to give a
demonstration of Sinn Féin's political strength and its power
of maintaining an armed resistance to the authority of
British law. Other 'outrages' for the week, says the review,
included fifty raids on mails, fourteen raids for arms, and
nine raids on the offices of the petty sessions clerks. Sums of
money amounting to over £10,000 were seized in the last-
mentioned raids. Arrests for 'outrages' and political offences
numbered forty-four for the week.

Quarry

On 17 May, the dead body of Martin Dermody, an ex-soldier of Kilmanagh, County Kilkenny, was found in a sandpit. Michael Quinn, also an ex-soldier, was found seriously wounded in the same location and he died the following day. They had been taken from their beds the night before by disguised and armed men who marched them to the quarry and shot them. Dermody had interfered with an IRA operation five days earlier

Marine

Corporal Ernest Williams, Royal Marine Light Infantry, stationed at Rosses Point, County Sligo, was returning by car from Sligo on 17 May when he was stopped by some men, taken to a shore near the road and riddled with bullets. His dead body was found later the same day.

Civilian workers

At 7.30 am on Monday, 20 May, three civilians were kidnapped by armed men who marched them away to a disused quarry about a mile and a half outside Cork city. They were put on their knees and shot. The three victims were: Daniel Hawkins (52); his son, Edward (29); and John Sherlock (35). Daniel Hawkins survived. Edward was married with three children. Edward worked as a labourer for the British military, and Sherlock as a civilian driver in the barracks. Both were ex-servicemen.

Polling day
RIC Sergeant Peter McDonagh, a native of Brookeborough, County Fermanagh, was shot dead in an ambush while cycling in a police patrol from Greencastle to Mountfield in County Tyrone. The rest of the patrol escaped uninjured. They had been going to arrange a polling booth in Greencastle for an election on Tuesday, 24 May.

Hospital case
John 'Hoppy' Byrne (45), disabled since childhood, was alleged to have been recognised on an RIC police raid at 16 Usher's Quay, Dublin, in which several Volunteers were arrested. He was shot but survived his injuries and was transferred to Jervis Street Hospital, Dublin. The following afternoon, 21 May, the IRA arrived at the hospital, arrested the porter, and went into the ward carrying a stretcher on which they placed Byrne. Patients thought they were medical staff. They took Byrne outside, put down the stretcher and shot him twice in the head.

Stoneybatter

An ex-soldier, Leslie Frasier/Frazer, of 9 Blackhall Place, Dublin, was coming out of a shop in Stoneybatter with another man on Sunday, 21 May, when they were approached by a group of armed men. Frasier's companion was told to 'clear off'. Frasier was then shot and he fell to the ground. He was shot twice more. He was removed to Richmond. Hospital but died at 10.30 pm. His name was believed to be amongst those of informers uncovered by documents seen in Dublin Castle.

Shoeing and informing

Patrick Briody, a shoemaker of Mullahoran, County Cavan, was taken from his wife and three daughters in the early hours of 23 May and was denied a request to get dressed. He was shot thirteen times, a few hundred yards from his home. He had been told to stop repairing boots for the RIC but did not heed the warning. He was suspected of giving information to the police.

Herrod

The badly decomposed body of Acting Quartermaster Sergeant Herrod of the South Wales Borderers was found by a fisherman on the evening of 24 May in the River

Blackwater, a mile from Navan, County Meath. The remains were brought to the mortuary. Herrod's hands had been tied behind his back with rope, his eyes covered with a handkerchief, and another handkerchief was stuffed in his mouth. His body had been weighed down with a 17lb stone held in place with a leather belt. The inquest found that Herrod met his death by strangulation inflicted by a person or persons unknown. A week earlier, Herrod, in civilian clothes, had left Navan Workhouse, where his battalion was stationed, for a walk and failed to return. Herrod was believed to be on intelligence duties when the IRA killed him on 16 May.

Postman

A patrol of military and police discovered the dead body of James Morrissey, a rural postman, in a field at Coolnahorna, County Waterford, on Wednesday night, 25 May. He died from wounds caused by a shotgun blast to the head and chest. A local postman, Morrissey was accused of being an informer and of mixing with Crown forces. An envelope on his body read, 'Spy and traitor. Others beware!—IRA.'

Cork

The dead body of Christopher O'Sullivan, an ex-soldier of Cork, shot through the forehead, was found outside the western suburbs of Cork city on Friday afternoon, 27 May. Intercepted mail indicated to the IRA that he was gathering intelligence for the British. He had left a note: 'Dear wife, I am going before my God.'

Mallow

Henry Fitzgerald, an ex-soldier, and his brother, Thomas, a railway gatekeeper, were shot dead on Saturday, 28 May, outside their house near Mallow. They were taken by a party of eight armed IRA men who called to the house in the early hours, walked them out the road and executed them as spies.

British Army horses

On Saturday, 28 May, when a groom was exercising two horses, the property of officers stationed at Dundalk Barracks, County Louth, he was confronted by armed men who shot the animals dead.

Sunday morning

An Ulster Special Constabulary police patrol was ambushed in Fivemiletown, County Tyrone, early on Sunday morning,

29 May. Constable Robert Coulter was shot dead. Another constable, James Hall, was seriously wounded and later died from his injuries.

'Weak mind'
The body of Daniel McCarthy, of Bantry, was found dead on the road at Ovens, near Ballincollig, County Cork, at 8.30 am on Saturday, 28 May, with a label pinned to his body bearing the words, 'Spies and informers beware! IRA.' There were eight bullet wounds in his chest and five in his head. McCarthy was said to be of 'weak mind and harmless'. He was seen coming out of Ballincollig Barracks. When the IRA interrogated him, he never spoke.

Bandsmen killed
'Seven British soldiers were killed and 21 were wounded in a mine attack at Youghal, County Cork, on May 30th at about 8.20 pm. A priest, a Reverend Roche, who was passing at the time was wounded. His driver received wounds from which he later died. The driver's name was Patrick Kenure.
'Three of the dead soldiers were band boys and three of the wounded were band boys. The lorry was completely wrecked by the explosion from the landmine.

'Dean Kellner sent a telegram to the military commandant expressing "horror at the tragedy and sympathy with the wounded".'

— *Irish News*

Twenty-one other ranks from the 2nd Hampshire Regiment were wounded in what was considered to be the IRA's most successful landmine attack during the Tan War. Father Roche and John [Patrick] Kenure were shot by panicking British soldiers, Kenure fatally wounded.

Inquiry

At the court of inquiry into the deaths of Corporal Whichlow, Lance Corporal Reginald McCall and the five bandsmen killed at a mine explosion at Youghal, the officer in charge stated that they were playing in the lorry while on their way to the rifle range. The band members were unarmed.

The mine was exploded by a battery from about seventy yards away. The court was of the opinion that this 'cold-blooded murder' was 'deliberately planned on account of the popularity of the band and regiment and that the murderers knew that the band was unarmed and contained many young boys'.

Cricket match

Kathleen Wright, a twenty-one-year old student, and her fiancé, George Herbert, went to watch a cricket match in College Park, Trinity College on 3 June in which one of the teams represented the military of Ireland. IRA men opened fire from Nassau Street, striking and killing the young woman, who died in the arms of George Herbert.

North Strand civilians

Andrew Hanratty (19) was killed when grenades were thrown at a military lorry at Newcomen Bridge, North Strand, Dublin, but missed their target and exploded on the footpath. There were no military casualties. Eleven other civilians were wounded.

Hospital visitor

Joseph Miller, aged fifty-nine, of South King Street, Dublin, died on Saturday, 4 June, in St Vincent's Hospital. He was shot the previous Sunday during an IRA gun and bomb attack on two military tenders as he was on his way to Harcourt Street Hospital to visit his dying wife. He survived for a week before succumbing to his injuries.

Band boys

Three unarmed band boys of the Manchester Regiment were playing a game of football near the barrack in Ballincollig, Cork, on 5 June. They were John Cooper (16), Matthew Carson (17) and Charles Chapman (17). They were chased by the IRA and found hiding in Kilcrea Abbey, where they surrendered without a struggle. They were taken to a house in Aherla, shot dead and then secretly buried in a field near Kilcrea. After the Civil War, Carson's father came from England looking for his son's remains and the three bodies were eventually recovered.

Tara Street

A fifty-two-year-old man, Charles Mullins, Sandwith Street, Dublin, was fatally injured by a metal splinter during a gun and bomb attack on an RIC lorry at the corner of Tara Street and Pearse Street on 8 June which wounded five policemen. Thirteen-year-old William Gorman, on his way to hospital to visit his five-year-old sister, also died in the IRA attack.

Secretly buried

Nineteen-year-old Private George Chalmers of the Royal Scots, an orphan from Edinburgh, was caught by the IRA in

Ennistymon, Clare, on 11 June as he went to meet a local woman he was courting. He was shot and secretly buried. His remains were not recovered until May 2018.

Reverend killed

Reverend James Finlay, Church of Ireland Dean of Leighlin, aged eighty, of Bawnboy, County Cavan, was killed by a blow to the head from a blunt instrument in the early hours of Sunday, 12 June. His home, Brackley House, was raided and set on fire, causing local and national revulsion. There was a rumour that the house was to be converted into a barracks. Reverend Finlay's name appears on a list of spies executed by the IRA.

New RIC recruits

Three weeks after joining the RIC, two ex-servicemen, Michael Brennan and John Frederick Smith, both in their twenties, were spotted in plainclothes drinking in a Dublin pub on 12 June. The two were taken out and brought to Rainsford Street, where they were shot dead. 'It wasn't much of a fight,' IRA Volunteer Donal Hannigan said. 'I killed two of the enemy.'

Farmer

A Protestant named Francis Boyle (38), living with his mother, and farming at Claremore, Fethard, County Tipperary, was found shot dead near his home on 14 June. Pinned to his back was a card with the words, 'Tried, sentenced and shot by IRA. Spies and informers beware!'

Fisheries inspector

The body of a fisheries inspector, James Kane (65), a retired RIC sergeant, was found on the road at Kilmorna, about three miles from Listowel, County Kerry, on 14 June. He was a widower with seven children. There were several wounds in his head and chest and he lay face down in a pool of blood. There was a handkerchief drawn over his face and attached to the body was a card with the words, 'Convicted spy. Let others beware!' Dublin Castle stated that Kane would have been prosecuting in a number of poaching cases at the next local petty sessions.

Civil bills officer

George Sackville Wallace (65), a civil bills officer in Cashel, County Tipperary, was shot dead by armed men on 14 June at a place called Hills, three miles from Cashel. Part of his head was blown away. The body was labelled 'Spy'. He left a wife and seven children.

Ballingarry

At 1 am on Wednesday, 15 June, Robert Healy, an ex-soldier, aged twenty-four and married, of Ballingarry, County Tipperary, was shot dead. He had been blindfolded and a label bearing the words 'Tried, sentenced and shot by the IRA. Spies and informers beware!' was attached to his body.

The letter

Mrs Potter, wife of Gilbert Potter, a district inspector in the RIC who was kidnapped on 22 April between Clougheen and Cahir, County Tipperary, received a letter from IRA Headquarters, Tipperary No. 3 Brigade, dated 27 April:

'To Mrs Potter, Cahir.

'Madam

'1. It is my sad duty to inform you that your husband, G. Potter, was legally executed yesterday.

'2. Your husband was charged with and found guilty of waging war against the Republic.

'3. We tried to arrange an exchange of prisoners. We offered to release your husband if the British Government would release Volunteer Traynor, who was similarly charged. Personally, I don't believe the offer went past Dublin Castle.

'4. Your husband was treated with the utmost consideration while a prisoner in our hands.

'I am yours—O/C.'

This letter was produced in court and Mrs Potter was given permission to presume the death of her husband.

Doubts

Patrick Darcy, a twenty-seven-year-old schoolteacher, who had two brothers in the IRA, was denounced as a spy by a local republican and accused of involvement in the arrests of two other IRA men who were killed in custody. He maintained that he was innocent and said he forgave his killers just before he was shot dead on 17 June in Doonbeg, Clare. For decades afterwards, doubts persisted about his guilt.

Sunday excursion

About 5 pm on Sunday, 19 June, an officer of the 2nd Worcestershire Regiment, while out driving and accompanied by three ladies, was held up by armed civilians at Carrickmines, Dublin. The officer tried to draw his revolver, was dragged from the car, shot and seriously wounded. He was then put back into the car and one of the women was forced to drive to the Dublin Mountains. The officer was then taken from the car and killed. He was Second Lieutenant A. D. H. Breeze, aged twenty.

British intelligence links

Two ex-soldiers, Michael Reilly and Thomas Cunningham, both married with families, were taken from their homes in Belmont, Offaly, and shot dead on 18 June. Cunningham had entertained military intelligence officers at his home. Reilly's wife did washing for the officers in the local barracks and Reilly occasionally received notes from soldiers which his wife claimed were just notices to collect laundry. She said her husband was shot dead 'because he was not a rebel'.

Bolton Street bombs

Michael Martin, aged four, Catherine Mahon, aged thirty-eight, and Elizabeth O'Brien, aged thirty, were all fatally wounded on 18 June when two bombs aimed at a patrol of RIC policemen and soldiers of the Wiltshire Regiment exploded in Bolton Street, Dublin. Six civilians, a policeman and seven soldiers were also injured. It later emerged that Elizabeth O'Brien's husband was in the IRA and that his unit had carried out the attack.

Chased

Three military officers, out walking in civilian clothes near
Fethard, County Tipperary, on a Sunday afternoon, were
encountered by two IRA men on 20 June, were chased and
dropped their weapons. Apparently, they accepted their fate.
They were blindfolded and shot dead at Castleblake. The
dead were Lieutenants Walter Glossop (21) and Robert
Bettridge (21), of the Royal Field Artillery, and Lieutenant
Toogood (20), of the Lincolnshire Regiment.

Earl kidnapped

On 21 June, the IRA raided Castle Bernard, west of
Bandon, County Cork, to capture and hold hostage the Earl
of Bandon, James Francis Bernard, against the lives of IRA
men in custody. When they couldn't find him they set fire to
the castle. But then he and his servants emerged from the
cellars, where they had taken refuge. The Earl, aged seventy-
one, was kidnapped and Castle Bernard was completely
burned down to its foundations. The Earl was released after
three weeks but was said to have never recovered from his
ordeal.

Just married

Constable George Duckham (21) was in plain clothes and returning from his wedding in England when he was captured by the IRA between Macroom and Millstreet. His body was left at the side of the road as ambush bait but local people fearing British reprisals buried it in Clashmaguire Bog.

Stray bullet

In a drive-by gun and bomb attack on Grand Parade RIC barracks in Cork city on 23 June, a young woman was killed and several civilians wounded. Josephine Scannell (19) was in an upstairs room at her sewing machine when a bullet came through the window and fatally struck her in the neck.

Train derailed by future Tánaiste

An IRA unit under Frank Aiken (later a Fianna Fáil Tánaiste) in Camlough, County Armagh, derailed a train on the Belfast to Dublin line at Killeavy. Carriages, the luggage van and a dozen cattle wagons tumbled down an eighteen-foot embankment, killing the train guard, forty-three-year old Francis Gallagher, a married man with three children, from 7 Colinpark Street, West Belfast. Three soldiers of the 10th Hussars and fifty horses were also killed in the attack. Gallagher was married with three children.

Grafton Street

Two Auxiliaries in civilian clothes were shot dead in Grafton Street, Dublin, shortly before 6 pm on 24 June. They had just left a restaurant after a cup of tea during a shopping trip when they were ambushed by a gang of men. The Auxies were George Warnes (28), Cranley Grange, Eye, Suffolk, and Leonard Appleford (28), Harold Wood, Essex. It later emerged that the IRA had intended carrying out multiple attacks with Thompson machine guns on soldiers in restaurants around the Grafton Street area at dinner time but were thwarted by increased military checkpoints which disrupted movements.

Councillor killed

Arthur Treanor, a forty-seven-year-old married man with five children, from Emyvale, County Monaghan, was taken from his home and shot dead as a 'spy'. Treanor was a member of the Ancient Order of Hibernians, which was opposed to the IRA, and had been a councillor on Monaghan Rural District Council. He had been warned about calling into local barracks. It was also alleged that he had walked out of a council meeting rather than vote for a resolution of sympathy for Terence MacSwiney and Kevin Barry. The IRA fined him £10—which his wife paid when men called to the farm. His wife was then assured of his safety but the men returned in the early hours of 25 June and shot him.

Mayfair

At 7 pm on Sunday, 26 June, two Auxiliaries, E. W. White and William Hunt, were having tea with their wives at the Mayfair Hotel, Baggot Street, Dublin, when armed men entered the dining room and opened fire, wounding Hunt, who fell to the floor. The gunmen rolled him over and shot him again at point-blank range. White was wounded.

Mass shooting

On Sunday, 26 June, about forty yards from the church gate in Kildorrery, County Cork, where they had been attending Mass, two RIC policemen were attacked by gunmen. Constable Thomas Shanley (30) fell to the ground, where more shots were fired at his body. Three-year-old Jeremiah Donovan and another Mass-goer were wounded and taken to hospital. The parish priest administered the last rites to Shanley whilst around two hundred worshippers knelt and prayed. Ryan escaped with a slight wound to his right wrist.

Dev's warning

Text of letter from Eamon de Valera to Lloyd George:

'Sir—I have received your letter. I am in consultation with such of the principal representatives of our nation as are available.

'We most earnestly desire to help in bringing about a lasting peace between the people of these two islands, but we see no avenue by which it can be reached *if you deny Ireland's essential unity* [my italics—Ed.] and set aside the principle of national determination.

'—E. de Valera.'

Visiting sister

RIC Constable Owen Hoey was shot dead at Forbes Lane, Dublin, on 28 June. He was in civilian clothes and had just left his sister's house when a number of men came up to him and shot him several times in the head.

Limerick

James Doherty, an ex-soldier pensioned from the British Army after losing an arm in World War One, was found shot dead at Athlumkart Bridge, Limerick, on 28 June. He had been abducted from his home four days earlier. A note was fixed to his clothing, part of which read: 'Men and women, spies and traitors beware.'

Dillon's Cross

Three unarmed soldiers from the 2nd South Staffordshire Regiment out walking on 27 June were attacked at Dillon's Cross, Cork, by armed men. One soldier was killed and one wounded; the other escaped.

Charleville

James O'Sullivan (17) and Patrick J. Sheehan (28) were found shot dead on the roadside at Coolasmuttane, Charleville, County Cork, on Wednesday, 29 June. Both men had been monitored by the IRA and were seen on one occasion leaving an RIC barracks by using the back wall. O'Sullivan was captured first and confessed. He was held for a fortnight until an opportunity arose to lure Sheehan, a carter, to a creamery with a delivery of coal. He was then abducted.

They were blindfolded and shot. Attached to each was a card: 'Convicted spy. Beware!—IRA.'

The RIC denied that either of the two men was an informer.

Lure

On 1 July, a patrol of seven RIC constables was sent to inquire into a robbery at a grocer's. This turned out to be a lure. The patrol was ambushed at Culleens on the main

Ballina to Sligo Road by about thirty armed men. Constable Carley was wounded in both arms. Constables John King and Thomas Higgins, who were leading the party, were captured. The men pleaded for mercy— but the IRA decided to shoot them. Their bodies were recovered by the RIC and military reinforcements.

The Limerick bus
RIC Constable Cyril Brewer, a native of London, his wife and infant daughter, arrived in Limerick by bus on 6 July and were spotted by IRA men, who opened fire. Brewer tried to escape by running through a shop and scaling a back wall but he was followed and was mortally wounded, dying the following day.

Died in fire
Gunmen seeking to set fire to a Navy & Army Canteen store demanded the keys from William Doran, the caretaker, who lived above the premises with his family. He denied having the keys. The gunmen then broke into the store, commandeered two cars and set the place alight. Doran's wife, thirty-four-year-old Bridget, trapped above, threw her ten-months-old baby to her husband and safety but she and her eleven-year-old stepson, John, could not escape and the pair perished in the fire.

Train gun battle

On 8 July, the IRA at Ballyfermot Bridge, between Inchicore
and Clondalkin in Dublin, attacked a passenger train which
was also carrying soldiers from the Gordon Highlanders.
Machine-gun fire was directed at the train, bombs were
thrown and petrol was poured on the wagons from the
bridge. Four civilians were injured. Fifty-seven-year-old John
Rossiter, a groomsman accompanying horseboxes with
animals that had raced in Bellewstown earlier, had his right
leg severed and he died later that evening. He was married
with nine children.

Linesmen

Draper Holmes, a forty-eight-year-old ganger with the Great
Northern Railway, was stopped by the IRA early in the
morning of 9 July, about a mile from Newry, County
Down. They were looking for B-Special police reservists
from Altnaveigh, some of whom also worked as linesmen.
Holmes put up a struggle and was shot dead. He wasn't a B-
Special but a unionist supporter.

Refused

Fifteen-year-old Bridget Dillon, whose father was a former policeman, refused to give water to an IRA party who called at the family farm in Kilcash, County Tipperary, at night-time on 10 July. The men tried to break into the house and a shot was fired, wounding Bridget who died of her wounds two hours later.

Prison Guards

Four unarmed soldiers who worked as guards in Cork Prison were out walking in their civilian clothes on the evening of 10 July when they were confronted by the IRA. They were taken to a nearby field and shot dead. They were Albert Camm (20), Harold Daker (20), Albert Powell (20) and Henry Morris (31), a widower with three children.

Body lost

Welsh fusilier William Williams died on 10 July after his motorcycle fell into a road crater dug by the IRA at Bunratty Bridge and he was flung into the River Shannon and drowned. His remains were discovered in 1925 before being lost again when the river flooded.

Wanted to serve

When it became known that seventeen-year-old William
Nolan from Friar's Walk, Cork, expressed an interest in
joining the RIC he was abducted and killed on 10 July.

*Although on 11 July 1921 the Truce was announced, and the
IRA campaign was halted, the IRA continued to defend
nationalist areas in the North, particularly in Belfast, which
suffered an onslaught before and after the establishment of the
six-county state.*

APPENDICES

Appendix 1

Béal na mBláther

Mick Timothy

An Phoblacht/Republican News, August 1984

Last Sunday, at Béal na mBláth in County Cork, the Free State Minister for Justice, Michael Noonan, upheld, as a glorious example for us to follow the memory of Michael Collins.

Shall we, for once, not be too proud or too self-assured to take the advice of this Fine Gael minister? Shall we follow the example of Michael Collins?

Collins undoubtedly had success and he had failure too. No one would surely have us follow the example of failure. That failure came when Collins was flattered and fooled by the crafty, smooth-talking British into betraying the cause he had fought for in exchange for false promises.

That led Collins into siding with the self-servers, the middle-class bandwagon-jumpers with a profitable stake in the country, and turning with British guns against his former comrades—a path that led to his own death at Béal na mBláth.

That was the failure of Collins as it is the failure of those who have come after him, and the reason why the task remains unfinished.

What then of his success?

Michael Noonan identified that success for us last Sunday by quoting with approval the words of Arthur Griffith:

'Collins was the man whose matchless and indomitable will carried Ireland through the terrible crisis. He was the man who fought the Black and Tan terror until England was forced to offer terms.'

But how, in fact, did Collins, as IRA leader, achieve this success which Michael Noonan would have us follow? How did Collins operate even before the Black and Tans arrived in Ireland?

For a start, he imported guns and money for guns from supporters in the United States. Yes, and robbed Irish banks and post offices for funds as well.

Shall we take Michael Noonan's advice and follow the example of Michael Collins?

Collins identified those who were the tools of British rule in Ireland and directed his men against them. And he targeted in particular the members of the RIC—those 'fellow Irishmen', often those 'fellow Catholics', those policemen doing their duty'.

How did Collins deal with them?

He had his men shoot them down without mercy; a bullet in the back, in the dark, on their way to or from Mass, when they were unarmed, or with their families — it mattered not to Collins. Many more native RIC men were killed than Black and Tan Brits.

Shall we take the advice of Michael Noonan and follow the example of Michael Collins?

How did Collins deal with the British military on the streets of Dublin?

By bomb and grenade; lie in wait secretly, throw it and run. And when there were civilian casualties, as there were—46 civilians dead and 163 wounded in one five-month period—they were the unfortunate casualties of war.

Shall we take the advice of Michael Noonan and follow the example of Michael Collins?

How did Collins deal with spies and informers and those seen to be too friendly with the RIC and Brits?

Take them out and put a bullet through their heads. Old or young, no matter. Leave a label: 'Spies and informers beware!'

Shall we take Michael Noonan's advice and follow the example of Michael Collins?

How did Collins deal with agents of British rule in Ireland?

He directed his squad against them *en masse,* riddled them with bullets in their beds one Sunday morning, next to their wives, in front of their children, without hesitation.

Shall we take Michael Noonan's advice and follow the example of Michael Collins?

What of the highest political representative of Britain in Ireland at that time, the Viceroy, Lord French? What of that old man?

Collins planned an ambush for him and when it went wrong was furious.

Shall we take Michael Noonan's advice and follow the example of Michael Collins?

And when the media condemned his methods as 'murder most foul', how then did Collins react?

He dispatched his men to the offices of the *Irish Independent* where they held the editor at gun-point, dismantled the entire printing machinery and destroyed it.

Shall we take Michael Noonan's advice and follow the example of Michael Collins?

And when the pulpits and episcopal seats of Ireland

reverberated with moral denunciations and threatened hell and damnation for the methods used by Collins?

He just ignored them.

Shall we take Michael Noonan's advice and follow the example of Michael Collins?

But, after all, Collins had a mandate at the ballot box to carry out his bloody guerrilla war.

Not so.

At the 1918 elections there was still a year before the first RIC men were to be shot down. Nobody was asked to vote for war.

But the election of May 1921, surely that endorsed such methods retrospectively?

Not so again.

You forget, do you not, that just like the SDLP in Fermanagh & South Tyrone 60 years later, the other parties were 'advised' to stand aside on this occasion. In 124 constituencies, the Sinn Féin candidates were returned entirely unopposed. Not so much elected as selected, you understand.

Shall we take the advice of Michael Noonan and follow the example of Michael Collins?

And even after Collins had blasted his way to the negotiating table, and even after the Treaty, he instructed his men in London to settle an old score with Sir Henry Wilson.

Shall we take the advice of Michael Noonan and follow the example of Michael Collins?

After all, according to Noonan:

'Our generation of the Irish owes more to Collins than to any other Irish hero.'

Or was last Sunday's commemoration in Cork not so much Béal na mBláth but rather Béal na mBláther?

Appendix 2

Background to the first edition (1985)
Brian McDonald

There was a time in the late 1970s when the mere expression of a nationalist (much less republican) position on events north of the border in the letters page of a newspaper was reason enough for the then Minister for Posts & Telegraphs, Conor Cruise O'Brien, to add your name to the list of those considered 'subversive'. While Section 31 of the Broadcasting Act had banned republican spokespersons from the broadcasting media, this period also saw the emergence of a culture of self-censorship within the print media. Meanwhile, politically-motivated historical revisionism was in its heyday, substituting new myths for old, selectively and subjectively using source material to rubbish Ireland's story of resistance to British rule.

While the great and the good had been more than happy to mount platforms in 1966 to mark and celebrate the rebels of Easter Week and their deeds, a decade later there was no state commemoration. Fearful that the public might make a connection between the story of that earlier period of struggle and the ongoing republican struggle in the Six Counties, the then Fine Gael/Labour coalition government decided to pull a veil over that period in our history.

The marginalisation of the republican viewpoint was made easier by the fact that Sinn Féin, through its abstentionist policy from Leinster House, posed no political threat to the two and a half party system that then characterised politics in the Twenty-Six Counties. The emergence of Sinn Féin as a political force in the Assembly elections of October 1982, and the subsequent election of Gerry Adams as MP for West Belfast, prompted a change in approach by the then Fine Gael/Labour coalition government of Garret FitzGerald. While they had always drawn a distinction between the 'Old IRA' and the contemporary IRA, a determined effort would be made to rubbish any suggestion that there was a historical connection between them. By extension, modern Sinn Féin could not be seen to share the legacy of Ireland's revolutionary past.

The campaign to divorce contemporary and historical republicanism began in earnest in October 1982 in response to an invitation by the organising committee of the Kilmichael Commemoration in west Cork to Gerry Adams, asking him to address the annual commemoration of the most successful IRA action of the Tan War. Determined to prevent Adams being directly associated with the famous ambush, Government and media put pressure on the committee to withdraw the invite and, when this failed, they pressured surviving veterans of the ambush to stay away. Defence Minister Paddy Cooney refused the usual permission for Defence Forces rifles to be supplied to the firing party at the event.

Despite cajoling and threats of violence, the event proved hugely successful, drawing the largest attendance for many years. To make matters worse, a close friend of Tom Barry, the IRA leader of the ambush, revealed that, prior to his death a few years earlier, Barry had voiced full support for the current IRA campaign.

The obvious discomfort of the Southern establishment at modern-day Sinn Féin representatives being in any way associated with the heroic struggle of the past prompted *An Phoblacht/Republican News* to publish a series of articles that exposed the 'good IRA, bad IRA' case being advanced by the establishment. A centrespread titled 'The hypocrisy of historical revisionism', published on 9 February 1984, provided a catalogue of just some of the actions carried out by the IRA between 1918-1921. This article provided the basis for what would later be published in *The Good Old*

IRA. Back then I wrote for *AP/RN* under the by-line Jack Madden. I'd graduated from University College Dublin's history department, a bastion of politically-motivated revisionism. I was assisted in my research by two others, Hugo Reavey and Fintan McPhillips, from my native Clones.

The research was thorough, using a range of sources. Besides trawling through contemporary newspapers, archival collections were consulted, including the papers of Michael Collins, Ginger O'Connell (who became prominent in the Free State Army after the Tan War), J. J. O'Donovan and others. Other related issues addressed by *AP/RN* during 1984 and 1985 included 'The Media and the Easter Rising', 'The Catholic Church and the Irish Revolution' and, on 4 October 1984, 'Gun-running to Fenit 1916'. This last article was published in response to the ludicrous claim by the then Labour Party leader, Dick Spring, that there was no comparison between Casement's attempted importation of arms in advance of the 1916 Rising and the attempted importation of arms by those captured on the Marita Ann off the same coast of Kerry just days earlier. Spring's speech followed the previous month when, in the course of another verbal onslaught against the 'men of violence', Justice Minister Michael Noonan told those gathered for the annual Michael Collins Commemoration at Béal na mBláth that the people of Ireland should 'follow the example' of Collins. This speech prompted a spirited reply by *AP/RN* editor Mick Timothy: in an editorial titled, Béal na mBlather, he described the deadly and effective campaign co-ordinated by Collins to destroy British rule in Ireland. Following Mick's death, this editorial would be reprinted as part of the introduction to *The Good Old IRA* [see Appendix 1, page 263].

Due to pressure of space, the original article cataloguing IRA actions during the Tan War had only included a tiny fraction of the hundreds of the documented incidents uncovered by the research conducted in early 1984. The relentless attempts to deny any equivalence between the modern and historical struggles led to a proposal being put to Sinn Féin Publicity Director Danny Morrison that the much wider database be published and issued to all media outlets, as well as being more generally available to the public. The pamphlet's publication in late 1985 prompted Vincent Browne, the then proprietor of Ireland's premier political magazine, *Magill*, to acknowledge that the facts presented could not be denied.

Acknowledgements

I'd like to thank those friends who read the manuscript and suggested a variety of amendments, among them John Hedges, my old friend from our days together editing *An Phoblacht/Republican News.* Of course, I owe a huge debt to Brian McDonald, Hugo Reavey and Fintan McPhillips whose initiative it first was to expose the hypocrisy of Fianna Fáil and Fine Gael legitimising the actions of 'the Good Old IRA' whilst denouncing the same resistance from a community which they had abandoned. Also, a big thanks to Danny Devenny who designed the original version (among a thousand other posters and pamphlets he put his creative mind to). Other readers and advisors whom I'd like to thank include the forensically-minded Niall Meehan, Tina Neylon, Andrée Murphy, Ciaran Quinn and Seán Napier.

I'd also like to thank Seán Mistéal for layout and jacket design and for Greenisland Press and Elsinor Verlag for the publication.

Ultimately, of course, the responsibility for the text is mine alone.

Index

Index

Index

Index

Index